HOUSE

— TO —

HOUSE

BOOKS BY LARRY KREIDER

Building Your Life on the Basic Truths of Christianity
(available in English and Spanish)

Building Your Personal House of Prayer

Discovering the Basic Truths of Christianity
(available in English and Spanish)

House to House

AVAILABLE FROM DESTINY IMAGE PUBLISHERS

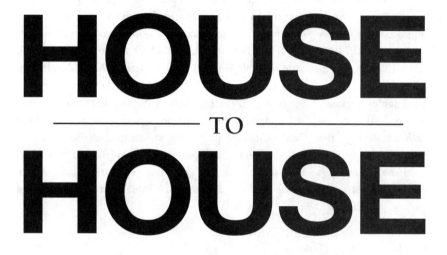

HOUSE ——TO—— HOUSE

GROWING HEALTHY SMALL

GROUPS AND HOUSE CHURCHES

IN THE 21ST CENTURY

LARRY KREIDER

DESTINY IMAGE® PUBLISHERS, INC.

P.O. Box 310, Shippensburg, PA 17257-0310

"Speaking to the Purposes of God for This Generation and for the Generations to Come."

This book and all other Destiny Image, Revival Press, MercyPlace, Fresh Bread, Destiny Image Fiction, and Treasure House books are available at Christian bookstores and distributors worldwide.

For a U.S. bookstore nearest you, call 1-800-722-6774.

For more information on foreign distributors, call 717-532-3040.

Or reach us on the Internet: www.destinyimage.com

Previously published as *House to House* by House to House Publications

ISBN 10: 0-7684-3057-7
ISBN 13: 978-0-7684-3057-8

For Worldwide Distribution, Printed in the U.S.A.

1 2 3 4 5 6 7 8 9 10 11 / 13 12 11 10 09

DEDICATION

*"...I have not hesitated to preach anything that would be helpful to you but have taught you publicly and from **house to house**. I have declared to both Jews and Greeks that they must turn to God in repentance and have faith in our Lord Jesus"* (Acts 20:20-21).

House to House is dedicated to my wife LaVerne, to our children, Katrina, Charita, Joshua, and Leticia, and to the hundreds of faithful small group leaders and house church leaders with whom we have had the privilege of serving during the past three decades.

Many of the spiritual principles outlined in this book were learned through the School of the Holy Spirit. And we are still learning with each step of faith. Many believers have given of themselves to serve our Lord Jesus in the building of the "underground church" throughout the world. To them this book is also dedicated.

But most importantly of all, this book is dedicated to the One who has promised us that He will build His Church...our Lord Jesus Christ.

ACKNOWLEDGMENTS

Special thanks to Karen Ruiz for her overall editorial assistance, Sarah Sauder for her oversight on this project, Hank Rogers for his assistance, Jackie Bowser for writing the thought-provoking questions at the end of each chapter, Steve Prokopchak and Brian Sauder for helping me clearly communicate what the Lord has placed on my heart, Lee Grady for his editorial help, Ron Myer for "covering my tracks" to give me the time needed to write, and many others who proofread this book. To the dozens of people who read the manuscript and offered valuable insights every step of the way, thank you.

And a very special thanks to those with whom we have been privileged to labor—the entire team, both at home and abroad, who have been so encouraging and supportive of my spending the time writing and rewriting this book.

TABLE OF CONTENTS

PART I
BACK TO THE BASICS OF
NEW TESTAMENT CHRISTIANITY

PART II
GRASSROOTS LEADERSHIP DEVELOPMENT

PART III
GOD POSITIONS US FOR THE FUTURE

FOREWORD

I am privileged to read several manuscripts each year before they are released to the public. I have the opportunity to give my opinions to the author and endorse the work for all of those who will read its pages. I usually read each manuscript by skimming through the pages to get the overall context, looking at each major heading, and then reading the key themes of each chapter. I also look forward to rereading the book after the publisher makes it available to the entire Body of Christ. However, this book by Larry Kreider was different. I found myself reading each word, and my spirit man leapt as I read each page. Even on the two plane rides when I was reading *House to House,* I heard myself say, "Oh God, I love this! Oh Lord, this is right and is the 'it' to capture this moment for where we, the Church, are going!"

House to House is the revolutionary book we need to change the course of the Church again. This book is a must for any grassroots movement. What is written here will help us produce the necessary changes for the Kingdom to advance in the future. *This book is visionary!* Larry communicates his vision, heart, and "come to Jesus meeting at the creek"! This book is *apostolic* in that the order that manages this vision looks like Ephesians 4 in the Bible! This book is *theological* because it traces the Church's development and success from a biblical standpoint! This book is *futuristic* and combines the history of the past with the future call to the Church to overcome! This book is filled with *methodology!* Larry shares failed approaches, as well as operational methods that work!

In the Hebrew Year 5769 and Roman Year 2009, the Triumphant Reserve began to reform and transform society in the midst of this chaotic, crisis-filled time! We have entered a season of the new wineskin. Like never before, we are in a season of divine alignment. God is setting in order His holy array! He is developing His order. He is pouring out His wine. Many would say that He does not pour out His new anointing if the Body is not prepared to receive the release of His power in a new way. I do not find that to be completely correct. In the history of the Church, on the day of Pentecost, there was no sufficient structure for the "new thing" that happened. God used homes to develop the structure. I weathered the latter 1960s and early 70s that were wild, unconventional, glorious, and devastating at times. There were few structures in the religious world that wanted the new converts that were finding the Lord during that time. The Jesus Movement was a true movement but had to move outside of the conventional church methodology; homes seemed to be the perfect solution.

The time has come again for a great new move of God to sweep the earth. Several years ago, the Lord asked me to help realign His Body to create a new order in preparation for this move to begin. He had revealed to me that we were entering a new war season, and in the midst of the season, there had to be a new alignment, a new method of gathering and "doing church." I initiated Zion Connect so individuals could connect functionally. I knew there were many in the Body of Christ who had been scattered in the past couple of decades. Also, there were many looking for the new wineskins that the Lord was developing in this season. He said, "Tell My people to be sure you are aligned somewhere! Develop a plan to gather the scattered sheep." At that point, the call of our ministry, Glory of Zion International, changed. We are a prophetic, apostolic ministry that ministers throughout the world. I have been used to help establish a worldwide prayer army over the last three decades. Now, the Lord seemed to be saying to me, "Help Me gather My people in a new way!"

All of us who are called to minister to God's people are having to be creative as we develop His wineskin for the future. I had been involved in the cell movement when I was on the staff of a Baptist church in the

1970s and 80s and had seen many of the pitfalls and benefits of cell ministry. After moving my family to Denton, Texas (where our ministry is located today), we connected with Robert Heidler. As he and I began moving forward together in ministry, we incorporated cell groups into our vision, knowing that small groups were key.

However, because of extensive travel and other demands, I lost sight of the call in the new millennium and our "cell groups" just rocked along. *However, when God speaks, things change and take a different identity!* I had found that the Internet and web-based communication were wonderful tools for connection and communication. I understood that many who had found their prophetic gifting being squelched in the traditional church needed to be reconnected while others in many areas around the United States and even internationally did not have viable churches at all. Therefore, if I could find these people, they could use their computers to connect in a new, functional way in their homes. By gathering in their homes and watching our webcasts to better hear what the Spirit is saying to the Church, the "scattered sheep" now have an avenue to hear and then pray for their territories in a new way. *With the web, I knew what I was to do. I am a connector and mobilizer. Once He said, "Gather," I was ready to do so.*

Church is a gathering where we fellowship. However, church is more than people gathered for fellowship. Church is a gathering to gain war strategies so we triumph against the enemy that Jesus came to destroy (see 1 John 3:8). Church is the viable organism that God uses to advance His Kingdom. The original warring unit that God designed was His family unit. I believe that is why the enemy attempts to destroy families and the concept of family by using mega-gatherings where no one seems touched. The functional connecting of giftings is just as important as territorial or local fellowship. Even though I travel as much as three weeks out of the month, I want to stay connected with my local church family. I also want to attend the prophetic prayer gatherings that go on during the week. I have a burning desire to stay connected, and our Internet webcasts have provided this opportunity.

Zion Connect was designed to keep the Body connected and communicating via the Internet so all of us could better develop and mature in our gifts. Many with intercessory, prophetic giftings now have a way to connect and can once again reach out to others around them and in their communities. Therefore, Glory of Zion has become a gathering place for many who are called to a more revelatory way of doing church. I encourage those who are connecting with us, and whose homes are their sanctuaries, to be part of local fellowships as much as possible, but to hear, pray, and move in a prophetic dimension that will bring transformation to their community. We encourage them in this new day of change to experiment with what God is doing. We have pastors on staff in Denton who are there to minister and help Zion Connected homes become vibrant with the glory of the Lord.

For us to see God's order, apostles must be first, prophets second, and then we can pastor and teach the sheep properly. This movement is much more than people finding Christ and needing each other. This is a movement with new order and authority. This is a movement that will see the world evangelized. We have begun to see a shift from scattered sheep to the triumphant reserve! We are seeing His family restored and becoming a viable, holy army in the earth. The works of Jesus are being done again, and with the ability to communicate around the world, I believe we are seeing the "greater works." Each gift in the Body of Christ that is resident in all who believe in the Lord Jesus Christ must come into the fullness of its God-designed destiny! The Kingdom of God is moving forward! To accomplish this requires all the ascension gifts to be aligned: apostles, prophets, teachers, evangelists, and pastors. A plan of dominion for "this age" has been released. I believe Larry has captured a portion of this plan for us.

*This book, **House to House**, will be sent to everyone who is connected with us! The amazing practical guidelines in the book will free many to look at their main resource, their home or dwelling place, and see how this place can become a sanctuary for many.* Larry Kreider has designed this book to help us stay on the edge. Revelation 12:10 is a central theme for those who understand *House to House*. This is a day of covenant and reorganization of resources. If we can grab hold of the revelation here and unselfishly use our resources as God's gathering place, we could see the Body of Christ multiply 30-, 60-, or even 100-fold!

Dr. Chuck D. Pierce
President, Glory of Zion International
President, Global Spheres, Inc.
Watchman, Global Harvest Ministries

FOREWORD

Larry Kreider has recently reorganized his book *House to House*, rewriting some of it to include house church ministry in the mix, along with cell group ministry. This update will make his last decade of experience impact the activity of church life for the next decade. The Holy Spirit is gently shifting the paradigms of God's people. It is astonishing to see the way old wineskins have started leaking and new ones have developed. More and more are realizing that the small group/cell group/house church is an expression of the literal Body of Christ on the earth today.

The real paradigm shift taking place in ecclesiology is the conviction that everything the people of God do is rooted exclusively in the life of the indwelling Christ. Another characteristic of the model expressed in this book is that it is a movement, not just a parish. Cell churches everywhere think globally, knowing that their ambassadors will all be "home grown" in the base church before being sent to plant new works.

Studies of people reveal that only 2.5 percent are innovators. Kreider is one of them. Innovators have the special capacity to see something as "real" when it is only theory and then to make it come to pass. It is painful to have to backtrack and try another direction. This book is the result of many of those cycles. It can save the reader much time in experimentation.

Larry's book joins the small collection of writings that can steer you on your journey and will be remembered as a pioneer's contribution to the family of God. Pick up a highlighter and begin to mark the pages that follow!

DR. RALPH W. NEIGHBOUR JR.
Houston, Texas

INTRODUCTION

It has been over 30 years since the Lord called my wife LaVerne and me into Christian leadership. In 1971, we helped start a youth ministry reaching out to unchurched kids in our community. From these seeds planted, the house-to-house strategy of DOVE Christian Fellowship International sprouted several years later. This book was originally written from the perspective of our experience with the new wineskins of small groups in a cell-based church and our commitment to church planting throughout the nations.

I have since revised it to accommodate the advent of new wineskins that are continuing to emerge. Today, in addition to cell churches, new "house churches" and house church networks are growing throughout America and in the nations of the world. This new kind of wineskin especially appeals to the younger generation. Like cell churches, house churches are relational, and all members are liberated to serve as ministers. However, house churches are different in that each functions as a real church.[1] Cell churches, while meeting in small groups during the week, are part of a larger unit—the local congregation that meets corporately each weekend.

I firmly believe that we need many kinds of churches to fulfill the Great Commission. From traditional churches to cell-based churches to new house church networks—the Lord will use all types to help bring in the harvest. The principles of small group ministry in this book apply to training leaders for house churches as well as for small groups in cell-based congregations. Although cell groups in local churches and house churches are instinctively different, there are many similarities, as you will see throughout this book.

Please note: some names used in this book have been changed to maintain privacy for the people mentioned. The personal illustrations and experiences that I share are (for obvious reasons) from my own personal viewpoint.

Use This Book as a Guide for Small Group or House Church Ministry

Much of what you read throughout *House to House* may serve as a guidebook to which you can refer in the days ahead. No one book has all the answers, but if you are a small group or house church leader, an assistant leader, or a potential small group leader, you will find that this book will guide you as the Holy Spirit builds the Church of Jesus Christ through you. If you sense that the Lord is calling you to labor with Him to build His Church from house to house according to this underground pattern, my desire is that the Lord will use these scriptural principles and practical suggestions to spur you on.

Please note that throughout this book, I use several terms interchangeably when referring to small groups of believers experiencing community, including: home groups, house fellowships, small groups, life groups, cell groups, house churches, micro churches, and simple churches.

Also note: In order to facilitate easier reading of this book, I will generally use the masculine gender when referring to leaders in the church. For the record, we firmly believe that women today are given a spiritual mandate to lead just as women in the early church labored as leaders.

—Larry Kreider
March 2009

PART

I

BACK TO THE BASICS OF
NEW TESTAMENT CHRISTIANITY

CHAPTER 1

What's an Underground Church?

Foreclosure on their house forced Jeremy and Megan to face the facts of Jeremy's problem with alcohol. Looking for a new start, they moved to south-central Pennsylvania from Long Island, New York. New to the community and feeling extremely lonely, one day Megan decided to take her nephew to a local park with hopes of making some new friends. Kathy, a young mother and small group leader in a local DOVE Christian Fellowship church, happened to be in the park that day and struck up a conversation with Megan.

Sensing Megan's loneliness, Kathy invited Megan to her home, to give Megan the opportunity to meet more people in the community. They exchanged phone numbers, and a few days later Kathy called Megan to remind her to come to their house the following Wednesday night. "Should we bring anything along to drink?" Megan asked.

"There's no need to bring anything," Kathy said. "We're just going to sing a bit and then have a Bible study."

When she got off the phone, Megan looked at her husband and said, "Hey, whadda ya know—it's a bunch of religious freaks!" But the lady in the park was so nice that Megan and Jeremy decided to go anyway. Jeremy liked the music, and they continued to go back. Within a few weeks, Megan made a commitment to follow Jesus Christ. Jeremy was happy about the change that he saw in his wife but hesitated to trust Christ himself.

However, a few weeks later, Jeremy had an encounter with the Lord while at his tree-trimming job. He was high up in a tree, cutting off a branch, when suddenly another falling branch hit him. It was a miracle he wasn't knocked to the ground. Knowing that someone had to be watching over him, he cried out to the Lord as he made a decision to follow Christ.

Before long, Jeremy and Megan began to serve as small group leaders at DOVE Christian Fellowship. Their story is just one of hundreds of stories that could be told of the lives we have seen the Lord dramatically change over the past 30 years.

It all started during the summer of 1971 when my fiancée LaVerne and I helped to start a youth ministry with a small band of young people who began to reach out to the unchurched youth of our community in northern Lancaster County, Pennsylvania. We played sports and conducted various activities throughout the week for spiritually needy youngsters and teenagers. This kind of friendship evangelism produced results, and during the next few years, dozens of young people came to faith in Christ with a desire to be incorporated into a local church.

Every Sunday night we took vanloads of these new believers to visit various churches in our community, because we wanted to help them find a local church of which they could be a part. After the church services, the entire group usually returned to our home for a time of praise, prayer, spiritual counseling, and just plain fun. Before long, some of the other leaders asked me to begin a weekly Bible study each Tuesday night for these new believers. Our desire was to teach them from the Scriptures what practical Christian living was really all about and assist them in being connected in a local church.

Those of us who served in this youth ministry were from various local churches, so we also attempted to help the new believers find their place in our congregations. Although the Christians in the local churches were friendly and helpful, something wasn't clicking. These young believers simply were not being incorporated into the life of the established churches in our communities. Some of the believers from unchurched backgrounds were getting married and starting families of their own, but they did not feel comfortable within the traditional church structures in our area.

The Need for Flexible Wineskins

We began to understand the answer to our dilemma when a church leader shared with us the following verses from Scripture. Although these Scriptures may have other applications, we sensed the Holy Spirit was using them to teach us about new church structures.

> *No one sews a patch of unshrunk cloth on an old garment, for the patch will pull away from the garment, making the tear worse. Neither do men pour new wine into old wineskins. If they do, the skins will burst, the wine will run out and the wineskins will be ruined. No, they pour new wine into new wineskins, and both are preserved* (Matthew 9:16-17).

This "new wineskin," we believed, was to be a new model of church structure, tailor-made to serve the new believers in Jesus Christ. And what better place to meet than in a home!

A wineskin is like a balloon. It needs to be flexible and pliable. Putting a new Christian (new wine) into an old structure can cause the structure to break, and the new Christian may be lost. New Christians should be placed in new structures that are flexible and able to encourage their spiritual growth.

The Lord promised to pour out His Holy Spirit *"in the last days"* (Acts 2:17). We believe flexible containers must be prepared for the great harvest that is on the horizon. In Second Kings 4:1-7, the widow brought all the containers she could find to prepare for the blessing God was pouring out.

New Christians should be placed in new structures that are flexible and able to encourage their spiritual growth.

Notice that the oil stopped when the containers were filled. Is it possible that the Lord is waiting for His Church to prepare the proper containers so He can pour out His Spirit again?

During the Jesus Movement in the 1970s, thousands gave their lives to Christ, but many were no longer living for the Lord a few years later. There were not enough "new containers" willing to be flexible enough to embrace these new believers, so many "fell through the cracks."

Now is the time to prepare for the coming awakening. We cannot force new Christians into our meetings—we must prepare new containers for the new oil. Forming new structures will enhance the Lord's commission to make disciples. We realize that many new types of containers (small groups, house churches, local congregations) are needed and must be formed.

Are You Willing to Be Involved in the Underground Church?

One day in 1978, I took a break from farm work and youth ministry duties in order to pray for a few hours. I was startled when I heard the Lord speak to me through His still, small voice. "Are you willing to be involved in the underground church?" He asked. I was shocked. The words that I heard in my spirit were distinct, even piercing!

What's an Underground Church?

When the Lord spoke to me, although the words were clear, I didn't understand what He was trying to tell me. My mind raced immediately to the Berlin Wall and the barbed wire fences that at the time surrounded the borders of many communist nations. I thought of the persecuted Church meeting underground in nations that opposed the Gospel. It still didn't make sense, yet I knew I had to respond; I was hearing the call of God—what would become a life call.

"Yes, Lord," I replied as tears formed in my eyes. "I am willing." I chose to obey, even though I didn't understand what it all meant.

Soon after the Lord spoke to me about the underground church, I asked some of my Christian friends if they would be willing to meet with me each week for the purpose of enhancing our own spiritual growth. Two men responded. We began meeting every week for prayer, Bible study, encouragement, and mutual accountability. Within the next few years this "house fellowship" grew, and we started to reach out to new believers. Soon our living room was filled to capacity.

With leadership established in the first group, eventually my wife LaVerne and I were commissioned out to help another couple start a second small group. These groups served as a place for new believers to be nurtured and taught the Word of God. We had no desire to start another church. We felt there were enough churches in our community.

Then one Sunday morning in January of 1980, while sitting in our local Mennonite church near Lititz, Pennsylvania, the Lord spoke to me through His still, small voice. As I was waiting for the service to begin, the Lord spoke these words clearly to my spirit, "It's time to start something new."

Although I had grown up in the Church of the Brethren, this Mennonite church was the congregation that I had become a part of when my wife and I married. I had married the pastor's daughter, served a year in the denomination's mission program on an island off the coast of South Carolina during our first year of marriage, and was a song leader for the Sunday services. While much of our time was taken up during the week reaching out to young people through a local para-church youth ministry, we had a genuine love and appreciation for God's people within our local church.

Nevertheless, I took this word from the Lord very seriously. After the service was over, a friend unexpectedly invited me to a meeting of church leaders the following day. At that meeting, I had the opportunity to meet the president of a local mission board who desired to see new churches planted. His encouragement spurred me on.

I told the other leaders of the two house fellowships that I sensed the Lord had called me to start something new. Others who were involved in youth ministry with us and still others in the Body of Christ in our area who had a similar vision came together to pray each week. It seemed clear that there was a need for a New Testament church that could be structured so it could be flexible enough to relate to believers from all backgrounds and assist them in their spiritual growth.

In the process of time, I slowly began to understand what the Lord had in mind when He asked me if I was willing to be involved in the underground church. An underground church is like a tree: its trunk, branches, and leaves are only half of the picture. The unnoticed half, the underground root system, nourishes the whole tree and keeps it healthy.

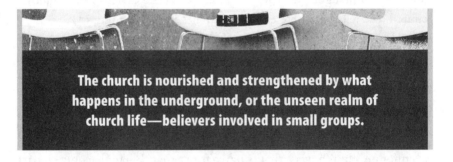

The church is nourished and strengthened by what happens in the underground, or the unseen realm of church life—believers involved in small groups.

The underground church, we began to realize, was to consist of believers gathered together through a structure of small groups meeting in homes to pray, evangelize, and build relationships with one another. In this way, each believer is made an active and vital part of the Body of Christ.

When every believer is nourished and healthy, the whole church is strong. As water and nutrients feed the tree by climbing up through the root system, so the church is nourished and strengthened by what happens in the underground, or the unseen realm of church life—believers involved in small groups. It was becoming clear that these relationships in small groups would not be an appendage of the church, but in actuality, they would be the basic building blocks of the church.

When Jesus cursed the fig tree, nothing appeared to happen immediately; however, the following day the tree was withered and dead. Probably the roots underground had dried up and died instantly, but it took until the next day for the leaves to wither and die due to the lack of water that came up through the root system.

The enemy seeks to destroy the church in the same way—from underground. He attempts to use broken relationships and to attack the lives of individual believers in order to weaken God's people. But when the part of the church that is underground is strong, then the whole church will be strong and continue to grow.

Time to Step Out in Faith

In October of 1980, our group of approximately 25 believers met for the first time for a Sunday morning celebration in a living room. Five families had been commissioned out of our local Mennonite church the week before to start this "new church." A small band of others also joined us at the inception of the new work.

We didn't have a name for our group until a woman in our group was praying and received a vision from the Lord. In this vision, she clearly saw four distinct capital letters with a period behind each letter [D.O.V.E.]. It appeared that the Lord was giving our new church a name. We sensed that DOVE was an acronym meaning, "Declaring Our Victory Emmanuel."

"DOVE Christian Fellowship" had officially begun. There was an air of excitement among us as we met in three separate home groups during the week, pursuing the vision that the Lord had given. But there were also times of pain. Within the first year, the three original house groups became two. Instead of the groups growing and multiplying, it seemed like we were going backward. We soon realized that we had a lack of clear leadership for the group, causing confusion.

False Humility

We had encouraged the believers in the first house fellowships to designate no one person as a leader but instead to choose a team that would provide co-equal leadership. Each house group had two co-equal leaders, and the church at large was led by six co-equal leaders. On the surface, this sounded good and noble; in reality, it was a manifestation of false humility. Underneath the surface, there was struggle.

It's funny to recall now, but with six of us leading, we discovered on one Sunday morning that we couldn't come to a decision about who should preach the Word in our celebration meeting. Since none of us was giving clear leadership, no one preached! It would be fine for no one to preach if the Lord was truly leading in this way; however, when it is by default, it causes confusion and stress among the Body of Christ. This type of leadership structure will either cause a move of God to stop, or it will slow it down until there is clarity regarding God-ordained leadership.

Harold Eberle, in *The Complete Wineskin,* says it like this:

> After observing many, many churches, I can personally tell you that no matter what form of government a church claims to have, there is always one person who openly or quietly holds the greatest influence over the church. Setting up the proper government is never a matter of keeping it out of the hands of one person, but putting it into the hands of God's person.[1]

Within the first year, this "leaderless group" came to the difficult realization that there was a need for clear leadership among us. Although we continued to believe that team leadership was important, we recognized the need for "headship" on each leadership team. Two spiritual leaders from our locality who had agreed to oversee and serve our fledgling group helped us through these difficult times. Two from the group of the original six co-leaders were set apart as leaders of the church and were ordained by a local denomination that was committed to supporting us during these early years. I was acknowledged as the primary leader of the leadership team.

During the next ten years our church grew to well over 2,000 believers scattered throughout communities in a seven-county area of Pennsylvania. These believers met in more than 100 small groups during the week and on Sunday mornings came together in clusters of small groups (congregations) in five different locations. The whole church came together five or six times each year on a Sunday morning in a large gymnasium or at a local park amphitheater for a corporate celebration. There was a real sense of excitement and enthusiasm about the things of God.

Whenever congregations renting facilities for Sunday-morning celebrations outgrew a building, we moved to a larger one, started a new celebration in another location, or started two or three celebration meetings in the same building on a Sunday. But the focus was not on the Sunday-morning meetings. The focus was on the church meeting from house to house throughout our communities each week in small groups.

Our goal was to multiply the small groups and celebrations and begin new Sunday-morning celebrations and new small groups in other areas as God gave the increase. We also found that by renting buildings economically, we had more money available to use for world missions. During these years, churches were planted in Scotland, Brazil, and Kenya. These overseas churches were built on Jesus Christ and on these same underground house-to-house principles.

We had embraced a new wineskin, and the Lord had grown us from a small fellowship of young believers into a church-planting movement. But there were storms ahead. We would learn we had to embrace not only a new wineskin but the Vine!

QUESTIONS TO THINK ABOUT
From Chapter 1

1. Describe a wineskin.

2. Using the tree as a picture of the present-day underground church, how does spiritual nourishment operate? Are you being nourished spiritually and nourishing others? Explain.

3. What is the most important or most appealing aspect of the underground church to you?

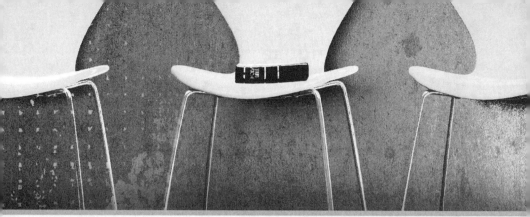

CHAPTER 2

Learning the Hard Way

About ten years into the life of our new church, storms began to mount. An undercurrent that constantly sapped those in leadership of strength and vision was surfacing. It was subtle—happening without us even realizing what was taking place—and it was difficult to put our fingers on it. I found myself increasingly making decisions that were based more on the desires of others than on what I really believed was the Lord's direction for us as a church.

People began to leave, not in vast numbers, but one family at a time. Even some of those who served in areas of leadership were leaving to find new direction in their lives. More and more, I felt pressed into a mold that was not the original vision God had given us.

Jim Petersen, in *Church Without Walls*, clearly describes some of what happened to us during these difficult years. Although he was talking about another fellowship, his story closely paralleled ours.

I have a friend who was a part of a team that set out to start a church.... The congregation was divided into house churches, each of which was assigned an elder who helped shepherd the members of that house church. Centralized activities were kept at a minimum for the sake of keeping people free to minister to their families and unbelieving friends. The weekly meetings were dynamic. I will never forget the first one I visited. People of all sorts were there, from men in business suits to ponytails. Many were new believers. The Bible teaching was down to earth, aimed at people's needs. I loved it. So did most everyone else who visited. The word got around and soon the migratory flock from neighboring churches came pouring in. Their needs consumed the energies of the leaders of this young church. Their wants gradually set the agenda. The inertia of the traditions of these migrants engulfed this very creative effort and shaped it accordingly.... So what's the problem, we ask? The problem is that the vision that the original team had for taking the church into society through the efforts of every believer was frustrated.[1]

Like this church, our vision, too, was frustrated. From the beginning, we had felt instructed of the Lord to reach pre-Christians and disciple new Christians. Developing new wineskins for new wine was a priority. But we found ourselves becoming more and more distracted by the many voices around us.

Another trap we fell into was adopting methods that worked in other churches, despite the fact that the Lord had not called us to these same methods. It has been said that we can never attempt to implement another man's program, unless we first learn to adopt his values. How true this became for our fledgling church. We learned the hard way that it is of utmost importance to adopt Christ's value system and hear from Him for the direction we should take as a church.

During the spring of 1991, we took time to pray, reevaluate, and seek God's face as we tried to come to grips with what the Lord was saying to us. Then, for more than a year, we were reevaluating or "maintaining" as a church.

This Isn't What I Signed Up For!

To be honest, during the spring of 1992, I was ready to quit. I felt misunderstood, and I wasn't sure if it was worth all the hassle. I told LaVerne one day, "If I get kicked in the head one more time (figuratively speaking), I don't know if I can get up again."

As the senior leader, I was frustrated, exhausted, and overworked. God had given me a vision to be involved in building the underground church, but in the last few years we had strayed from that original vision. My immaturity as a leader, lack of training, and my own inability to communicate clearly the things that God was showing me led to frustration. In a misguided attempt to please everyone, I was listening to dozens of voices who seemed to be giving conflicting advice and direction. I felt unable to get back on track. I was tired and was encouraged to take a sabbatical—a Sabbath rest from the ministry, time out to hear God more clearly.

So, I took the summer off to unwind, spend time with my family, and just enjoy life. It took me a while, but I really began to enjoy myself and even got into painting and wallpapering our house. My wife would describe that completed chore as a miraculous move of God! It definitely was a much needed change of pace.

During the last few weeks of the sabbatical, I spent some extended time at a cabin in the mountains. One morning I went out for a jog, and in a totally unexpected way, I had an encounter with the living God. After I returned to the cabin, I immediately sat behind my word processor (the name used for the early laptops) and typed in the occurrence that I had experienced. I didn't want to lose it or exaggerate it. I share it here to encourage all those who have at one time lost their vision and need the Lord to gently and lovingly nudge them back on track.

Crossing the Creek, No Turning Back

I had an amazing spiritual experience this morning. I went out for a jog, and I took a road that I am totally unfamiliar with. After jogging for a while through the countryside and then on a winding dirt road that took me through the woods, I came upon a creek (small river) that crossed the road, and my jogging came to a screeching halt. I was ready to turn around and go back when I heard a still, small voice within me tell me, "Take your shoes off and cross over the creek barefooted." I sensed that I was on holy ground.

In my flesh, I really didn't want to cross. I was not accustomed to going barefooted, and the thought of taking off my shoes and crossing the creek and getting my feet all muddy and perhaps stepping on a sharp stone really wasn't my cup of tea. But I continued to hear a voice deep within my spirit telling me to take off my shoes and cross over. I then began to understand with my spirit that the Lord was asking me to take a step of obedience and faith and cross over the creek barefooted (which was a sign of humility). This was not just a natural creek, but it also had deep spiritual significance for my life and for DOVE Christian Fellowship. The Lord was asking me to cross the creek in faith and in humility, and allow the water to wash away all of the hurts, expectations, fears, insecurities, and ways of doing things from the past so that the Lord could teach me fresh and anew for the future.

I obeyed the prompting of the Holy Spirit and took my shoes off and slowly walked across the "river" to the other side. It was a holy experience. A cleansing from the past took place deep in my spirit.

As I took this step of obedience, I sensed that others who were called to serve with me in leadership would need to do the same thing spiritually—walk across the creek in humility and allow the water of the Holy Spirit to wash them clean of many of the hurts, mind-sets, and expectations of the past. The Lord has called us from the wilderness to the promised land of Canaan. We must forget what is behind and press on to what the Lord has for us in the future.

I asked the Lord if this meant that we should change our name as a church. The response that I got was, "Your name didn't change when you crossed the creek, so why should the name change?" The change is in the spirit. It would be possible to change the name and nothing would change in the spirit. The Lord's desire, as I understood it, was for us to move on from a Moses mentality to a Joshua mentality.

Moses and the people of God walked "in a circle" for 40 years. Joshua had a clear mandate from the Lord to go into the Promised Land and take it back from the enemy. Moses majored on maintenance, while Joshua led an army! Each member of the army had clear areas to champion and to conquer; however, they were all committed to walking together to fulfill the purposes of the Lord.

I realized that I was called (along with those who were willing to cross the creek with me) to take the people of God into the Promised Land. In reality, in the same way that Joshua fulfilled the original vision that was given to Moses at the burning bush, I now believed that the Lord was calling me to fulfill the original vision that He gave me years ago when He asked me if I was willing to be involved with the underground church, and then a few years later when the Lord asked me to start something new. I knew I was committed to fulfilling the original vision the Lord gave to me in the late 1970s and in January of 1980.

Beware of the Dogs

I walked for a while barefooted and then sat down to put my shoes and socks back on. As I continued to walk down this road that was totally unknown to me, I had a few other significant experiences. First of all, the road took me into unknown territory. Less than a half mile up the road I had to walk by a mobile home. There were two dogs barking at me, one on either side of the road. The one was really close to the road and was a ferocious-looking guard dog. At first, I was fearful, but I knew that I was making the right decision. I just smiled and spoke gently to the barking dog. It hit me as I walked by that there was certainly nothing to fear. Both of these dogs were chained and could bark and make all of the noise that they wanted, but they still could not touch me or harm me in any way.

I believed that as I and others took this step of faith and each of us individually in the spirit made a decision to cross the creek, there would be some "barking dogs" (words spoken, perhaps harshly, against us), but it didn't matter; the enemy could not touch us. God knew our hearts, and He would vindicate us.

As I continued to walk, it was as if a whole new world opened up before me. The fields were beautiful, and it was a sheer delight to walk along these country roads. I had a clear sense that I was walking in the right direction, but in reality, it was a real step of faith. I had never been here before in my life. I believed that this was clearly symbolic of the future. We would walk in the direction that we believed the Lord wanted us to walk and yet have to totally trust the precious Holy Spirit for direction. I believed there would be a tremendous sense of peace as we trusted the Holy Spirit in this way.

The Joy of Building

The next thing that happened I saw as extremely significant. I passed an old Methodist church building. A brand-new building was being built on the backside of the same property. There were all kinds of people hustling and bustling around, working together on this project. The roof and the vinyl siding was on. What was so amazing to me was that the workers were women, teens, and men all joyfully working together to fulfill a common purpose—building the new church building. Along with the men, I saw women and a teenage girl with a nail bag tied around their waists. As I absorbed this scene before me, I felt the excitement and the joy and the expectancy within the people. I again sensed the still, small voice within me saying, "This is what it is going to be like as you have crossed the creek, and others cross the creek with you. There shall be much joy."

Just as these people were working together to build a physical building, the Lord was calling together a company of His people to work side by side to build His spiritual building. And in the same way that these workers were inexperienced in the eyes of the world, the Lord showed me that He would use those who appeared to be inexperienced in the eyes of the church to build His spiritual house. These workers were also using new lumber to build this building, and the Lord was going to require of us to use new lumber (new Christians) in the building of this spiritual house.

I had a renewed sense that we would experience a working together to fulfill the Lord's purposes that would be much greater than anything that we had ever experienced.

I knew I could not minimize the wonderful things that the Lord had done in past years. But truthfully, whenever we begin to be too nostalgic, we have a tendency to forget the negative things that have happened in the past and only concentrate on the positive. I now believed the Lord had wonderful plans for those who were willing to forget the past and press on to what He had in the future.

And sure enough, the road that I traveled by faith brought me back to the cabin. I would never forget this experience. It was worth taking off for the three-month sabbatical just for this spiritual experience. *Thank You, Father, for bringing me to that river to cross!*

I now had renewed faith and vitality to press forward in the calling God had given to me—to be involved in co-laboring with the Lord through building the underground church using small groups. I had crossed the river.

Back on Track

This incident was a major breakthrough in my life and in the life of DOVE. I repented for not properly fulfilling the charge God had given me 12 years before. He had given me and others the mandate to build the "underground church" by focusing on the formation of new wineskins for the new believers that were being brought into the Kingdom, and we had become sidetracked. Nevertheless, the Lord is good. Even though we had wandered from what He had called us to do, He heard our cries for forgiveness, and we received His cleansing.

Despite our many mistakes, the Lord has remained ever faithful. By His grace, we got back on track as a church family and continued working with Him to fulfill His call to build the underground church. As a leadership team and as a church, the Lord gave us the grace to again walk together in unity to fulfill His purposes. We are grateful to the Lord for giving us another chance.

We Decided to Give the Church Away!

Early on as a church, we believed the Lord was calling us to train and invest in His people, so we had the expectation that many believers serving in small groups would eventually have their own spiritual families (new small groups and new churches they would plant). We realized the importance of constantly training people in order to give them away. How do we give people away? As people are trained, they are released (or given away) to start new churches. In a business corporation, we say people have reached a *glass ceiling* when they can go no further in the corporation. They may have the potential and talent, but there is nowhere for them to advance. Multiplying people and allowing them to move out on their own affords limitless potential.

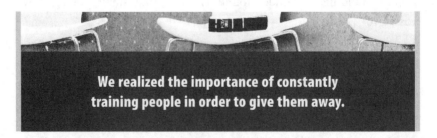

We realized the importance of constantly training people in order to give them away.

It became clearer to us that in order for DOVE Christian Fellowship to accomplish what God had in mind for us, we needed to adjust our church government and be willing to give the church away.

How do you give a church away? It's similar to giving a daughter away to be married. When our oldest daughter Katrina was married, we realized we had spent 21 years giving her our time, resources, love, encouragement, and finances. We had made this investment in her to give her away to a young man who would be her husband. We had trained her to give her away.

The Transition

At DOVE, we had often made the statement, "The only thing that is constant is change!" The good thing about change is that it often provides an opportunity for us to learn to trust the sovereignty of God more fully. We certainly had the opportunity to trust in His sovereignty when we realized God was calling us to change our existing church structure once again. We began to recognize that the Lord had called us to be an international family of churches and ministries, an "apostolic movement" if you will, and we took steps to make the transition.

An "apostolic movement" is comprised of people with various gifts who share common vision, values, goals, and a commitment to plant and nurture churches and ministries worldwide. An apostolic movement has God-given authority and responsibility to serve, train, equip, release, and protect the people, ministries, and churches throughout the movement, all the while advancing the Kingdom of God. We were about to grow into a family of churches and ministries with a common focus: a mandate from God to labor together to plant and establish church-planting movements throughout the world.

On January 1, 1996, after more than two years of preparing for transition, our one large small-group-based church in Pennsylvania became eight self-governed churches, each with its own leadership team. We formed a leadership team we called an Apostolic Council to give spiritual oversight to DOVE Christian Fellowship International (DCFI), and I was asked to serve as its international director.

We also realized our need for input from outside the DCFI family to provide the Apostolic Council with advice, counsel, and accountability. So a team of "recognized spiritual advisors" (spiritual fathers in the church-at-large) was formed to provide direct and personal accountability.

The newly formed Apostolic Council gave each church leadership team the option of becoming a part of the DCFI family of churches and ministries or leaving DOVE and connecting to another part of the Body of Christ. After clearly explaining the options and giving opportunity for prayer and input, each of these eight churches expressed a desire to work together with us to plant churches throughout the world and became a part of the DCFI family. The majority of the overseas church plants also joined the DCFI family of churches and ministries.

We decided to call these churches "partner churches." We became a movement of churches partnering together to fulfill the Great Commission of reaching those who do not know Jesus and making disciples locally, nationally, and internationally.

This transition was not easy for many of us. I enjoyed being the "senior pastor" of a mega-church with the security it brought. Those of us on the leadership team and staff of DCFI had to walk in a new level of faith. The finances we had received week after week from the tithes of this one local church were now given to each self-governing church. In some ways, it was almost like starting over. Yet, since the transition, we experienced the faithful provision of the Lord again and again as we walked in obedience to Him.

An Apostolic Movement Leads by Relationship

We have found this new model provides a safe environment for growth and reproduction. This new model emphasizes leading by relationship and influence rather than hands-on management and control from the top.

The Apostolic Council members were responsible to give clear vision and direction to the entire movement as they spent time in prayer, the Word, giving training and oversight, and initially mentoring local church leadership. By developing supportive relationships with local church pastors, they influenced the pastors but did not have direct authority to make local decisions.

In each church, it is the senior leader and his/her team who lead the local church. They have leadership gifts to equip believers to become ministers who serve people. The leadership team is responsible for direction, protection, and correction in that local body. They make decisions for their church with the input and general affirmation of those they lead.

Today, the Apostolic Council is an International Apostolic Council and has trained and released regional Apostolic Councils throughout the world. These Regional Apostolic Councils give basic oversight to church leaders in their region, but each local church leadership team is responsible to train the believers in their church. In this way, each church has its own identity while embracing the same basic values as the rest of the DCFI family.

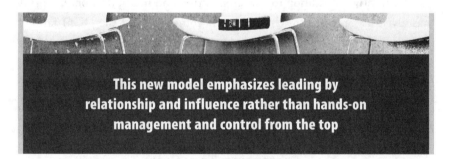

This new model emphasizes leading by relationship and influence rather than hands-on management and control from the top

The multiplication process continues as each church gives away the people the Lord has given to them. Otherwise, a bottleneck to future leadership occurs.

As one large, cell-based church, we were always intent on training a new generation of church planters and leaders. So, an entire family of self-governing churches better suited our goal of mobilizing and empowering God's people. In this way, everyone—individuals, families, small groups, house churches, congregations, and churches—can fulfill His purposes at the grassroots level.

We have come to believe that every church needs to have a God-given vision to plant new churches. This gives so many more of us a chance to fulfill God's individual call to us.

Broadening Our Focus

Although DCFI has always had a call to plant new churches from within, we were encouraged by various spiritual leaders to make it possible for other churches with like values to become a part of the DOVE family of churches. One day, the Lord spoke to my heart a message that has since broadened our focus when He revealed, "I have many orphans in My body, and I am calling you to adopt some of My orphans."

I knew He was calling us to open our hearts to churches that shared the same vision and values that the Lord had given to us that did not have spiritual oversight and apostolic protection.

Currently, in addition to church planting and multiplication, the Lord has given us a process for churches to become a part of the DCFI family. After going through a one-year relationship-building "engagement" period, churches throughout the world with similar values and vision are partnering with the DCFI family. Today, various apostolic teams in different regions of the world serve churches that want to partner with the DCFI family in their part of the world.

Partnering Together

Our transition from one large church to a family of churches allowed the old structure to die so we could experience the new—a network of churches partnering together. At the time of this printing, there are currently more than 150 churches partnering with the DCFI family from the nations of Barbados, Brazil, Bulgaria, Canada, Guatemala, Haiti, India, Kenya, New Zealand, Rwanda, Scotland, Peru, the Netherlands, Uganda, and the United States. The Lord has taken us on an amazing ride during the past few years.

House Church Networks

Like our early beginnings, we are again sensing that the harvest is upon us. The Lord, like a great magnet, is drawing people into His Kingdom. Since new wineskins eventually get old, many who have been believers for years are becoming dissatisfied with life as it is in their present church structures. God's people are again thirsting for new wine and new wineskins. The Lord is renewing and refreshing and reviving thousands of His people all over the world. He is requiring us to provide new wineskins again for the new wine, as He brings in His harvest.

We are already seeing evidence of some of these new kinds of wineskins. For example, house churches are sprouting up throughout the nations. China, especially, has the most strategically organized house church movement in the world. House churches often meet in homes like cell groups, but they are very different. Cell groups usually function as a complementary ministry to the larger Sunday church meeting, whereas a house church is the church itself—a complete little church that is usually connected to a house church network for encouragement and accountability. Some house churches are related spiritually to a community church or a mega-church.

Some house churches, as they grow, become small-group-based. For example, a new house church begins as one group, but wise leaders often train more leaders within the group to lead small satellite groups within the house church. So then, one house church may be comprised of several small groups. House churches are encouraged to network to maintain accountability and share resources when they find themselves in the same geographical area.

Some house church networks and cell-based churches look almost alike; they are a modern-day hybrid between the two models. But it really doesn't matter, because the most important thing is that people are coming to Christ, being discipled, and experiencing community and are intentional about fulfilling the Great Commission.

We are convinced that as we continue to reach those who do not yet trust Jesus in our generation, many new kinds of churches are needed.

Traditional community churches and mega-churches will coexist and network with the newer house churches, and God will bless all three! For more on house churches, read my books, *Starting a House Church* and *House Church Networks.*[2]

Learning From Our Mistakes

Of course, over the years, we have learned vital lessons from our experiences and our repeated mistakes. We desire to be candid about our victories and our losses. Hopefully, it will keep you from making some of the same mistakes, or at least you will learn from ours.

In many ways, it feels like the longer we walk out this vision, the less we know. And yet, the Lord is faithful to continually teach us. We are constantly learning. He faithfully teaches us how He can build His Kingdom through us. We desire to share with others what God has shown and is showing us because He is a creative God and constantly gives new insights to His people. We want to emphasize that we do not believe we have "cornered the market" on how God will move in our communities. We are well aware that God is using many types of churches and ministries to advance His Kingdom into the 21st century. Our prayer is that we all work together, listening to and depending on the Holy Spirit to direct our steps.

Starting with the next chapter, we will begin looking at the challenge you and I face in coming to understand God's priorities for our Christian lives. This is the single most important thing we can ever do before getting involved in ministry of any kind.

QUESTIONS TO THINK ABOUT
From Chapter 2

1. How does "change" give us the opportunity to trust God more fully?

2. How can adopting the methods of another group be detrimental to our church?

3. How is the Lord bringing your church together as a company of people who work in unity?

CHAPTER 3

God's Priorities

Often, our natural tendency is to look for formulas and methods to fulfill the Lord's plans. However, the more we grow in the Lord, the more we realize that our way of thinking with our natural minds is often not at all what the Lord has in mind. So before we get into some of the basic principles that we have learned about small group and house church ministry, let's begin with God's priorities.

Ecclesiastes 4:12 tells us, *"A cord of three strands is not quickly broken."* The three strands that we believe form the core of the Christian life are *prayer* (knowing God), *evangelism* (reaching those who do not know Jesus), and *discipleship* (training new believers).

Prayer—Knowing God

God has called us to trust Him, first and foremost! Matthew 28 tells us that Jesus appointed a certain place to meet with His disciples. And when they saw Him, they worshiped Him.

Then the 11 disciples went to Galilee, to the mountain where Jesus had told them to go. When they saw Him, they worshiped Him; but some doubted. Then Jesus came to them and said, *"...All authority in heaven and on earth has been given to Me. Therefore go and make disciples of all nations, baptizing them in the name of the Father and of the Son and of the Holy Spirit, and teaching them to obey everything I have commanded you. And surely I am with you always, to the very end of the age"* (Matt. 28:18-20).

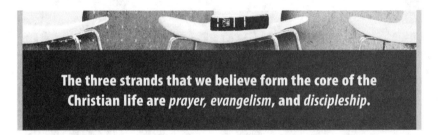

The three strands that we believe form the core of the Christian life are *prayer, evangelism*, and *discipleship*.

Jesus has called us to meet with Him and worship Him each day. The Lord tells us in John 17:3 that eternal life is to know Him. Our number-one priority must be to trust Him personally through time spent with Him each day, or small group ministry will become just another church program.

Dr. Paul Yonggi Cho is the pastor of one of the world's largest churches in Seoul, Korea. Dr. Cho has spoken to thousands of pastors and church leaders in America during the past years. He spoke at our church conference in Lancaster, Pennsylvania, several years ago and said that American pastors are attentive when he speaks on biblical principles that will help their church grow, but when he begins to teach on prayer and communion with the Holy Spirit, the pastors put their pencils down and stop taking notes. They lose interest. Be advised—the spiritual principles and guidelines outlined in this book will only be effective as long as we are in love with Jesus and are communing with Him daily!

Often when I speak at churches and conferences, I am not able to take my wife LaVerne with me. I find great joy in searching through my luggage for a special love note that she has hidden in my bags. I love reading those notes, because I'm in love with her. If I no longer desired to read those notes, it would be a warning light that my love for her is waning. Do you look forward to reading your love letters from Jesus? That is what the Bible is all about. It is filled with love letters from the God who loves us.

Jesus says in Matthew 4:4, *"Man does not live on bread alone, but on every word that comes from the mouth of God."* I need a fresh word from the Lord every day. If I am living on last week's manna, I will begin to get weak and even sick spiritually. Only healthy Christians will have something to give to others. And there is no substitute. We must cultivate our relationship with our Lord Jesus every day. If your prayer life needs a boost, I would like to encourage you to read my book entitled *Building Your Personal House of Prayer,* and experience an extreme makeover for your prayer life![1] The God-given principles in this book have radically changed my personal prayer life.

Evangelism—Reaching Those Who Do Not Know Jesus

Jesus spent much of His time with the tax collectors and the sinners of His day. His heart went out to those who did not live the way God wanted them to. The people who hated Jesus were not the sinners but the scribes and the Pharisees, the religious leaders. We need to be careful to not allow ourselves today to focus more on church politics, personal opinions, and self-preservation than on the priorities of Jesus.

The Bible says, *"... The reason the Son of God appeared was to destroy the devil's work"* (1 John 3:8). The works of the devil are everywhere. Our communities are filled with broken lives, fear, abuse, broken relationships, perversion, the murdering of unborn children, materialism, and lust. Jesus came for the purpose of destroying these works!

We must understand that our heart motivation for being involved in small group or house church ministry must be the same as that of our Lord Jesus—to destroy the works of the devil. Jesus is the answer to every problem. He is the great Redeemer. He came to restore completely every man, woman, and child who will open up their hearts and lives to Him. The Scriptures tell us, *"...How can they believe in the one of whom they have not heard?..."* (Rom. 10:14). We are commissioned by our Lord Jesus Christ to reach those who have not placed their trust in Him. Small group and house church ministry is one of the spiritual tools to assist us in fulfilling this mandate from the Lord.

Jesus told His disciples in Matthew 28 to *"Go,"* knowing that all authority had been given to Him in Heaven and on earth. He promised to be with them always, just as He will always be with us. Often Christians do not sense the Lord's presence with them. Could it be they are so caught up in the cares of this world that they feel unable to obey the commandment to go and explain the Good News of Jesus with those who have not yet believed in Him?

Lord, we need a revival. We need to get our priorities in line with Your priorities.

Discipleship—Training New Believers

Jesus commands us in Matthew 28:19-20 to *"...go and make disciples of all nations, baptizing them in the name of the Father and of the Son and of the Holy Spirit, and teaching them to obey everything I have commanded you...."* Unless we have a clear understanding that making disciples is near the top of God's priority list, small group and house church ministry will be just another religious program.

Jesus had a vision to revolutionize the world—person to person, house to house. Out of the multitudes of His followers, He appointed only 12 to be His disciples.

He appointed 12—designating them apostles—that they might be with Him and that He might send them out to preach (see Mark 3:14).

He took special time with three of them: Peter, James, and John. And John was clearly the disciple whom Jesus loved.

By living closely with His disciples, day in and day out, He gave them intense training, demonstrated His miraculous power, explained His parables, and answered their questions.

A disciple is a learner, an apprentice. Jesus provided His disciples with innumerable opportunities to practice and exercise the things He taught them. He poured His life into them by close, daily contact for three years. As we observe Jesus interacting with these 12 men, we see a model of what could be regarded as the first small group in the history of the Church.

The Lord commands us to go and do likewise. Whatever He has taught us, we are to teach to others. This not only applies to Bible knowledge but to practical Christianity. The most effective way for you to teach a young husband how to love and honor his wife is for *you* to love and honor *your* wife. The best way for you to teach another Christian how to have a clear financial budget is for you to show him how *you* set up a budget. If you believe the Lord has called you to teach a new Christian to pray, then pray with him! We teach others by modeling biblical truths with our own lives.

The Bible gives many examples of discipleship. Paul the apostle took young Timothy with him as a disciple (see Acts 16). Later, Timothy was sent out to do the same: take the truths that he learned from Paul and impart them to others (see 2 Tim. 2:2). Moses had Joshua as his disciple for 40 years, preparing Joshua for leadership. Elijah found Elisha and became his mentor. The list goes on and on. The Lord is restoring the truth of loving discipleship to His Church today. He has called us to make disciples.

We like to call this "spiritual parenting." God's intention is to raise up spiritual parents who are willing to nurture spiritual children and help them grow up in their Christian lives. In this way they are making a spiritual investment as they see others' potential in Christ and make themselves available to discipling them. This is a fulfillment of the Lord's promise to *"turn the hearts of the fathers to the children, and the hearts of the children to their fathers…"* (Mal. 4:6). Spiritual children need to have this kind of spiritual parents in their lives providing the character they need, telling them they are valuable, that they are gifts from God. Parents need to put expectation into children's hearts so they believe in themselves. In my book *The Cry for Spiritual Fathers and Mothers,* I reveal what happens if spiritual parenting does not take place:

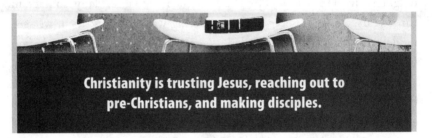

Christianity is trusting Jesus, reaching out to pre-Christians, and making disciples.

Too often, in today's church, a Christian believer is encouraged to participate in church services, Bible studies, para-church organizations or evangelistic ministry in order to bolster his faith and "grow strong in the Lord." The theory is that the more teaching from God's Word and interaction with believers, the more spiritually mature he will become. As important as these involvements may be, such a faulty supposition leads to inhaling message after message, book after book, tape after tape, seminar after seminar, in order to fill a void for real relationship.

A believer becomes fat spiritually and fails to interpret what he is learning so he can pass it on to others. He does not know how to meaningfully and sacrificially impart his life to others because he has never been properly fathered. Without a role model, he remains a spiritual infant, needing to be spoon-fed by his pastor or other Christian worker.[2]

Christianity is not just sitting in a pew or padded chair each Sunday morning, looking at the back of someone's head. Christianity is trusting Jesus, reaching out to pre-Christians, and making disciples. This must be the motivation of our hearts in order to fulfill effectively the Lord's purposes for us as believers in Jesus Christ. You will discover the three strands of prayer, evangelism, and discipleship woven throughout these pages; they will surface again and again.

"I'm ready!" you say. "I understand the challenge to make disciples, and believe that small groups of believers are an effective way to build the Church. But exactly what does the Bible tell us about small groups and house churches? What is the biblical plan of training through small groups of believers?" Read on!

QUESTIONS TO THINK ABOUT
From Chapter 3

1. What priority does prayer have in your daily life?

2. How recently have you discussed with another person what Jesus means to you?

3. What does being a disciple mean to you? In what ways are you discipling others? In what ways are you being discipled?

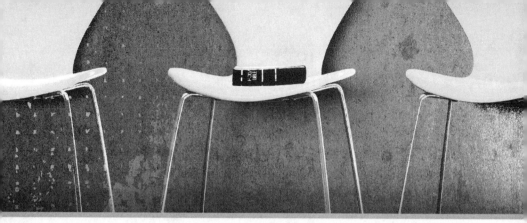

 CHAPTER 4

A Biblical Vision for Small Groups and House Churches

To be most effective to experience Christian community and the Lord building His Church through us, we believe that it is God's plan for us to follow Jesus' model of training through small groups and house churches. Just as a cell is one of the smallest units in the physical body, sometimes the term "cell groups" is used to denote the small units of the local church where relationships and personal growth take place. In this book we will mostly use the term *small groups,* although some call them by various names, including *cell groups, home groups, house fellowships, house churches,* and *life groups.*

Small groups of believers committed to one another give everyone an opportunity to get involved. In small groups, each person has the opportunity to begin to fulfill the purpose God has for his life. The small group is the place where he can receive training, instruction, and encouragement

    57

as he reaches out to his friends and neighbors with the Good News of Jesus Christ.

We have used the small group model to build God's Kingdom from the inception of DCFI. Small groups are not simply a program of the church; they are a place where people have the chance to experience and demonstrate New Testament Christianity built on relationships, not simply on meetings. In small groups, people share their lives together and reach out with the healing love of Jesus to a broken world. Our vision as a church movement is to *"build a relationship with Jesus, with one another, and to reach the world from house to house, city to city, nation to nation."* Since the principles of God's Word are applicable and adaptable to any culture, nation, or people group, we believe the guidelines and principles found in this book will be helpful to you no matter where you live as you reach the world for Jesus from house to house.

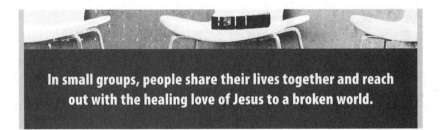

In small groups, people share their lives together and reach out with the healing love of Jesus to a broken world.

In addition to this book on small groups and house churches, I recommend another comprehensive training manual I've co-authored with Brian Sauder that gives the tools you need to design and build the biblical cell church and house church network entitled *Helping You Build Cell Churches.*[1]

The House-to-House Principle

The Scriptures tell us in Acts 2:41 that *"those who accepted his message were baptized, and about three thousand were added to their number that day."*

How could the 120 disciples in the upper room possibly have taken care of 3,000 new believers? Part of their secret is found in Acts 2:46-47 (NKJV):

> *So continuing daily with one accord in the temple, and breaking bread from **house to house,** they ate their food with gladness and simplicity of heart, praising God and having favor with all the people. And the Lord added to the church daily those who were being saved.*

God's people gathered at the temple and met in small groups in homes. *"They devoted themselves to the apostles' teaching and to the fellowship, to the breaking of bread and to prayer"* (Acts 2:42). They began to minister to one another and to those who were not yet followers of Jesus, and the Lord kept adding to the church daily! In Acts 20:20, the apostle Paul declares to members of the church at Ephesus, *"...I have not hesitated to preach anything that would be helpful to you but have taught you publicly and from **house to house."***

The letter that Paul wrote to the Christians in Rome was written to believers in Jesus Christ who met in people's homes. In his letter to the Romans, Paul indicates that one of these groups met in the home of Priscilla and Aquila:

> *Greet Priscilla and Aquila, my fellow workers in Christ Jesus....Greet also **the church that meets at their house**...* (Romans 16:3-5).

Paul also sent his greetings to the household of Aristobulus and the household of Narcissus (see Rom. 16:10-11). When Paul wrote to his friend Philemon, he expressed his greetings to the church in his house, *"...To Philemon our dear friend and fellow worker, to Apphia our sister, to Archippus our fellow soldier and to **the church that meets in your home"*** (Phil. 1:1-2).

Periodically, down through the ages, the church has lost the New Testament component of meeting in small groups in homes of individual believers and has placed an emphasis on the church as it meets in large buildings:

> It was in 323 A.D., almost three hundred years after the birth of the church, that Christians first met in something we now call a "church building." For all three hundred years before that, the church met in living rooms! Constantine built these assembly buildings for Christians not only in Constantinople, but also in Rome, Jerusalem, and in many parts of Italy, all between 323 and 327! This then triggered a massive "church building" fad in large cities all over the Empire.[2]

"Temple ministry" is beneficial for corporate worship, teaching, and celebration, but we believe that the Lord wants us to get back to seeing the Church as people, not as a place where believers meet each weekend. Our homes, places of business, schools, and other circles of contact provide excellent places for the Church to meet as we infiltrate our spheres of influence with the Good News.

What Was the Early Church Really Like?

T.L. Osborne, in his book *Soul-winning Out Where the Sinners Are,* tells the story of a possible conversation with Aquila in Ephesus, from the Book of Acts:

> "Good evening, Aquila. We understand you're a member of the church here. Could we come in and visit for a while?"
> "Certainly. Come in."
> "If you don't mind, we would like for you to tell us about the way the churches here in Asia Minor carry on

their soul-winning program. We read that you have been a member of a church in Corinth and Rome, as well as this one here in Ephesus. You should be very qualified to tell us about evangelism in the New Testament Church. If you don't mind, we'd like to visit your church while we're here."

"Sit down, you're already in the church. It meets in my home."

"You don't have a church building?"

"What's a church building? No, I guess we don't."

"Tell me, Aquila, what is your church doing to evangelize Ephesus? What are you doing to reach the city with the Gospel?"

"Oh, we already evangelized Ephesus. Every person in the city clearly understands the Gospel.... We just visited every home in the city. That's the way the church in Jerusalem first evangelized that city (see Acts 5:42). The disciples there evangelized the entire city of Jerusalem in a very short time. All the other churches in Asia Minor have followed that example."[3]

The church of today should take a lesson from the early church. Today's church has tried to reach people for Christ in our communities with extravagant church programs and 21st-century methodology. While such methods have their place, they can never substitute for personal relationships formed in the context of genuine Christian community.

A couple at a DCFI church began a small-group ministry in the heart of a nearby city. A man who has lived in this city all his life shared an observation that illustrates our point. He noted that many of the city churches have moved to the suburbs, while others have sought to promote programs encouraging city dwellers to come in. He was grateful to see the heart of this one couple and their work to move in among the community and develop relationships in order to share that God loves us and sent His Son so that we can find forgiveness and new life through Him.

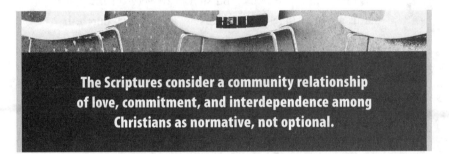

The Scriptures consider a community relationship of love, commitment, and interdependence among Christians as normative, not optional.

It's not too late to get back to basics and allow God to build His Church through New Testament relationships built through community. The Scriptures consider a community relationship of love, commitment, and interdependence among Christians as normative, not optional. Let's strive for this kind of community that the early Christians understood. They understood that their faith gave them a distinctive identity that they shared with other Christians.

Living Stones

The Bible calls us "living stones." Each believer has been made alive through faith in our Lord Jesus Christ.

As you come to Him, the Living Stone—rejected by men but chosen by God and precious to Him—you also, like living stones, are being built into a spiritual house to be a holy priesthood, offering spiritual sacrifices acceptable to God through Jesus Christ (see 1 Pet. 2:4-5).

The Lord builds us together with other Christians into a type of spiritual house or community. Christianity is practical. Who are the other living stones the Lord has built you with?

Do you know that as living stones we can demobilize the devil as we obey the living God? Imagine a large stone wall made up of thousands of stones mortared together. These thousands of stones are made up of clusters of stones that touch one another. Can you imagine how frightening it would be if each of these stones were alive and all decided to walk toward you *en masse?* That is how the devil feels when, as Christians, we pull together, realize God has called us to minister to one another, and obey the prompting of the Holy Spirit to destroy the works of darkness.

Each (living) stone can only touch a small group of other believers at one time. These believers are knit together in small groups through relationships as they are united in the Lord. Ten people who are of one mind and heart can have a tremendous impact on the kingdom of darkness. The devil would like to get us alone, to isolate us, leaving us without the support of our brothers and sisters in Christ.

In small groups, we can interact meaningfully with a few other people (Christians and those who have not yet received Jesus) through encouragement, prayer, and practical service. As each small group or house church obeys our Lord Jesus, the entire congregation or house church network has a powerful effect on our communities as we minister in Jesus' name. It's important to remember that the "ministers" Paul speaks about in the New Testament are not only the pastors or leaders—they include all the believers!

> *And He Himself gave some to be apostles, some prophets, some evangelists, and some pastors and teachers, for the equipping of the saints for the work of ministry, for the edifying of the body of Christ* (Ephesians 4:11-12 NKJV).

God has called every believer to be a minister. He calls the leadership gifts of apostles, prophets, evangelists, pastors, and teachers to teach and train all believers how to minister. You and I, average, down-to-earth believers in Jesus, are called to tend to others on Jesus' behalf. This ministry becomes quite effective in a small group setting.

Learning From History—the Methodist Revival

I have had the privilege of proclaiming the Good News of Christ on six continents during the past few years. Amazingly, in almost every nation that I go, I find a Methodist Church building! Some of my Methodist friends tell me that many of these buildings serve as memorials to a past revival. What happened?

Howard A. Snyder, in *The Radical Wesley,* says it like this:

> John Wesley [the founder of the Methodist Church] saw that new wine must be put into new wineskins. So the story of Wesley's life and ministry is the story of creating and adapting structures to serve the burgeoning revival movement. After 30 years, in 1768, Methodism had 40 circuits and 27,341 members....By 1798, seven years after Wesley's death, the totals had jumped to 149 circuits with 101,712 members. By the turn of the century, about one in every thirty Englishmen were Methodists.[4]
>
> A key to the Methodist revival was the accountability that each of these new believers found in small groups. Wesley called them class meetings.
>
> The classes were in effect house churches...meeting in various neighborhoods where people lived. The class leaders (men and women) were disciplers.
>
> The classes normally met one evening each week for an hour or so. Each person reported on his or her spiritual progress, or on particular needs or problems, and received the support and prayers of the others....According to one author it was, in fact, in the class meeting "where the great majority of conversions occurred."
>
> The class meeting system tied together the widely scattered Methodist people and became the sustainer of the Methodist renewal over many decades. The movement was in fact a whole series of sporadic and often geographically localized revivals which were interconnected and spread by the society and class network, rather than

one continuous wave of revival which swept the country. [Classes joined together to form a society.]

Without the class meeting, the scattered fires of revival would have burned out long before the movement was able to make a deep impact on the nation....

Now here is the remarkable thing. One hears today that it is hard to find enough leaders for small groups or for those to carry on the other responsibilities in the church. Wesley put one in ten, perhaps one in five, to work in significant ministry and leadership. And who were these people? Not the educated or the wealthy with time on their hands, but laboring men and women, husbands and wives and young folks with little or no training, but with spiritual gifts and eagerness to serve....

The system which emerged gave lie to the argument that you can't build a church on poor and uneducated folk. Not only did Wesley reach the masses; he made leaders of thousands of them.[5]

Slowly the Methodist believers began to put more of an emphasis on the Sunday morning church meetings in their buildings. As they de-emphasized the accountable relationships they had in their class meetings, the revival movement began to decline. God, help us to not make the same mistake in this generation! Let us learn from history that small groups and house churches have often served to fan revival throughout church history:

The ember that has rekindled movements of renewal ever since [the first century] is the cell group or "micro-community," as church historian Richard Lovelace calls the small group of believers that meets for prayer and support. As we seek to ignite a discipling movement in our own time, we must place the local prayer and support group concept at the very center of our strategy. The great reformer Martin Luther proposed that widespread spiritual renewal should take the form of *ecclesiolae in ecclesia*—little churches within the church.[6]

Tradition, Tradition!

Tevye, the patriarch in the classic motion picture *The Fiddler on the Roof,* loved tradition. If something has worked in the past, most people, like Tevye, are happy to continue on in the same way. The old adage, "If it isn't broken, it doesn't need to be fixed," satisfies many Christians today as they continue on in old patterns of church structure.

Although tradition tells us that believers should meet in a church building on Sunday mornings, according to the Scriptures the believers in the New Testament appear to have met in homes on Sunday mornings. Church history tells us that the believers met on the first day of the week.[7] But since the emphasis seemed to be on the house-to-house ministry and they didn't have their own buildings until about 250 years later, it seems reasonable to believe that the believers met in homes on Sundays.

We are not implying that congregations of believers shouldn't meet in a building on a Sunday morning. Our culture is accustomed to Christians gathering in a church building every Sunday—and there's nothing wrong with it. Nevertheless, we should ask the question, "Do we meet together in this way because the Holy Spirit has directed us to or because tradition has dictated it?"

Certainly, not all tradition is wrong; some traditions are godly and good. When traditions take on a life of their own, however, we may be in trouble, because we begin to trust a method rather than the Living God. Even small groups and house churches can become legalistic and traditional if we trust the method rather than allowing God to keep us flexible and open to His leading.

I look forward to the day when we can be so flexible that we will allow a church building to be utilized every day of the week. One congregation (cluster of small groups) could use the building on a Sunday morning. Another group could use it on Sunday night. Six other groups could use it the other six nights of the week. A group could even use it on Saturday morning. Imagine the same building being used by nine different congregations or house church networks! That's divine efficiency!

The believers could meet in small groups in homes on Sunday mornings. All of the money that is saved on renting and maintaining buildings could be given to missions and to the poor. Believers could meet together on a Sunday evening as a small group or house church and then meet as a congregation or house church network during a night of the week or one or two times each month. Of course, if houses are large enough, some congregations could have their regular meetings in homes.

With the recent global financial crisis of 2008, which is the worst of its kind since the Great Depression, the church in the 21st century may indeed have to downsize in light of these economic realities. In economic times like these, the value of small groups and house churches is especially appealing because they do not require large buildings to maintain.

Ralph Neighbour, in *The Seven Last Words of the Church*, makes some important observations about the church's dependence on buildings:

> Churches in the United States now own in excess of $102 billion in land and buildings. I am not picking on my denomination, but simply using it as an example: We will spend far more than $50 million this year simply to pay the interest on church mortgages. This profit by bankers from churches represents an investment which is several million dollars more than the amount to be invested by those churches for all home and foreign mission causes.[8]

Some years ago, our leadership team did a study from the Bible on the use of the tithe. To our amazement, we could not find even one reference in the entire Bible that encouraged using tithe money for buildings. The references that were given showed us that tithe money was to be used for supporting people, and then offerings were to be taken for buildings. Although most of the money that DCFI has spent during these past years on buildings has been on rent instead of on mortgages, we realized that in some cases we were spending too much of the tithes on buildings. Without becoming dogmatic regarding this principle, we must continue to take a close look at how we are spending the Lord's money so that we can see the church built effectively from house to house.

The Jethro Principle: Delegate Authority and Responsibility

Moses was wearing himself out by continually listening to and solving the disputes and dilemmas that arose among the Israelites. He was weighed down by the responsibilities that came with serving more than 3 million people. The Israelites were burdened by having to wait day after day for Moses to hear their case.

This reminds me of many pastors today. Many church leaders are nearing burnout, as they try all by themselves to juggle the crushing ministry responsibilities of the church.

God gave Moses, through Jethro, wisdom to rule so that he and the people would not be worn out. Jethro suggested a simple solution: Able men were to be selected from among the people to listen to any problems which arose, solve the ones they could handle, and pass on the most difficult cases to Moses.

> But select capable men from all the people—men who fear God, trustworthy men who hate dishonest gain—and appoint them as officials over thousands, hundreds, fifties and tens. Have them serve as judges for the people at all times, but have them bring every difficult case to you; the simple cases they can decide themselves. That will make your load lighter, because they will share it with you. If you do this and God so commands, you will be able to stand the

strain, and all these people will go home satisfied. Moses
listened to his father-in-law and did everything he said
(Exodus 18:21-24).

There would be one judge for each 1,000 people. Moses would appoint
ten additional judges under him, each in charge of 100; and under each of
them would be two judges, each responsible for the affairs of 50 people.
Each of these would have five judges beneath him, each counseling ten
persons. Only the most severe or perplexing problems got all the way up
to Moses, who alone had the God-given abilities to handle them.

We do not believe that it is necessary to set up a legalistic system in
the church that looks exactly like the structure that Moses used; however,
we are convinced that we need to see the church from God's perspective
and use the wisdom He has given us in determining its structure. Our
God set the sun and the moon and the stars in place: He is a God of
order.

The early apostles understood the principle of delegation that Moses
had used many years before. During the great awakening that took place
in the Book of Acts, the apostles soon found it necessary to delegate
authority and responsibility to others so that they could concentrate on
their top priority—prayer and the ministry of the Word.

So the Twelve gathered all the disciples together and said,
"It would not be right for us to neglect the ministry of the
word of God in order to wait on tables. Brothers, choose
seven men from among you who are known to be full of the
Spirit and wisdom. We will turn this responsibility over to
them and will give our attention to prayer and the ministry
of the word" (Acts 6:2-4).

Many times today, those in primary leadership in the church are so
caught up in management that they do not have time to pray and give
clear direction to the work of God. Applying the Jethro principle to the

local church would result in the delegation of authority and responsibility to believers on the "front lines" of ministry, who are best prepared to make such decisions anyway. Unless pastors and Christian leaders can release responsibility and authority to the servant-leaders at a small-group level, this principle will not work. Although local pastors in a cell-based church are responsible before the Lord for God's people in the small groups, the small group leaders must be released and trusted with the care of the people of God within their group.

When Dr. Cho from Seoul, Korea, was at our church in south-central Pennsylvania for a pastors' conference, I talked to him about the need to release local leadership in a small group setting. I will never forget his response. "Many pastors are threatened," he said. "They are afraid to release their people." It is my observation that this "fear" stems from our personal insecurity. If, as a senior pastor, you are threatened by the release of leaders who will minister to and lead small groups, then house to house ministry will not work for you.

Let My People Go

Moses gave Pharaoh the mandate of the Lord: "Let My people go!" I believe that the Lord is setting every believer free to be an "able minister of the new covenant."[9] May every spiritual leader maintain his security in the Lord and take the risk to release the people of God to minister to others.

Once servant-leaders release people to minister, the Church will grow by leaps and bounds, as it did at the first. But be prepared: with growth comes growing pains; with risk comes both success and failure. Even in the midst of inevitable setbacks, however, be encouraged, for failure is part of the process.

In the next chapter, we take a look at the very important role spiritual parents can have in developing and training spiritual children within the small group and house church setting.

QUESTIONS TO THINK ABOUT
From Chapter 4

1. What are some practical and financial reasons for limiting the number of big church buildings?

2. Explain the "Jethro principle."

3. What happens when pastors begin to release the people they oversee?

CHAPTER 5

Spiritual Parenting

Some Christians do not really grow to their full potential in God because they never had a spiritual father or mother to help them grow up spiritually. Jesus invested the three years of His earthly ministry in the lives of 12 men. It was key to the success of His ministry—fathering His spiritual children.

As I travel, I find a desperate need for spiritual fathers and mothers. I meet men of God who are used mightily of the Lord in the nations. They have a tremendous anointing as they minister to thousands. But when I talk to them in private, they express their need for a spiritual father. I have felt the same need in my own life on various occasions.

New Christians desperately need spiritual fathers and mothers. True spiritual leaders are willing to be spiritual parents to young Christians. One of the pastors who serves a local congregation at a DCFI church in Pennsylvania told me that when he received Christ in his mid-20s, a 77-year-old man from his local church took him under his wing and discipled him. It made all the difference for this future pastor's spiritual maturity.

All of us are called to be spiritual parents to someone—maybe a "pre-Christian." Small groups and house churches are a part of God's plan to establish spiritual fathers and mothers for the harvest of new believers who are going to be birthed into the Kingdom of God.

New parents seldom feel equipped. They learn by doing. It was scary for us when our first child was born. It may be scary for you to take the step of faith to become a spiritual parent to someone the Lord brings into your life, but it is a step of obedience that will bring eternal benefits.

Emily, a single girl from a DCFI church and only a baby Christian herself, explained what God had done in her life to Debbie, a young mother. When Debbie accepted Jesus, Emily took her along to her cell group. Cell members introduced Debbie to Jean, a mature Christian willing to spend extra time with Debbie explaining Scriptures, encouraging her, and simply being a friend. When Debbie's Jewish parents disowned her for becoming a Christian, Jean and the cell group helped her through those early difficult months. Over the next year or two, Jean discipled Debbie, rejoicing with her as God brought her victoriously through spiritual and physical crises. Debbie's spiritual journey started when a young Christian took a step of faith and shared Jesus, and then God provided a more mature Christian (a spiritual mother) to invest time in Debbie's life to help her along the way.

Training and Releasing People

At DCFI, "spiritual parenting" is a very important philosophy in releasing each believer in ministry.[1] Local church leadership is trained and encouraged to delegate authority and responsibility for ministry to the believers within the small groups and house churches. As elders empower small group and house church leaders to freely serve God's people by giving them responsibility and authority, the Lord releases every believer to be a minister.

We encourage leaders to take the risk of empowering and releasing small group and house church leaders to minister to others by performing water baptisms, serving communion, praying for the sick, giving premarital and post-marital counseling, discipling new believers, reaching out in evangelism, and providing missions opportunities.

A major aspect of small group and house church ministry is preparing and training future spiritual fathers and mothers. I will never forget the experience of having our first baby. I had faithfully attended prenatal classes with LaVerne, where I learned how to coach. But when the contractions started, reality hit me. We were going to have a baby! I just didn't feel like I was ready; I was too young. We had never done this before. I felt like telling LaVerne, "Couldn't you just put it on hold for a few months until we are ready for this?" But waiting was not an option. She was ready to give birth, and our brand-new baby girl was born.

A major aspect of small group and house church ministry is preparing and training future spiritual fathers and mothers.

It really felt strange being a "papa." We had never been down this road before. But somehow, with the faithful advice of trusted family and friends, it all worked out. That was many years ago.

When this "baby" girl got married, we gave her away. She had gone from being a baby, to a teenager, to an adult. And now, she is a parent and is preparing the next generation.

When it comes to spiritual parenting, many potential spiritual parents go through the same emotions and fears. "How could God ever use me to be a spiritual parent? What if I can't do it properly? Am I really ready for this?" But as they are encouraged to take a step of faith and obedience, they begin to experience the joy of becoming a spiritual father or mother. They have the satisfaction of training and releasing others for eternity.

Only a dysfunctional parent will try to hang on to his children and use them to fulfill his own vision. Healthy parents expect their children to leave their home to start their own families. Healthy spiritual parents must think the same way. This generation of Christian leaders are called to "give away" many of the believers in their churches to start their own spiritual families—new small groups and new house churches and new congregations.

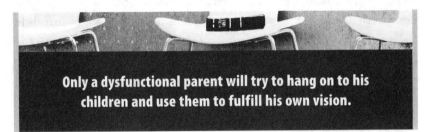

Only a dysfunctional parent will try to hang on to his children and use them to fulfill his own vision.

According to the Bible, there are three different types of people in our churches: spiritual children, young men, and fathers. First John 2:12-13 tells us, *"I write to you, dear **children**, because your sins have been forgiven on account of His name. I write to you, **fathers**, because you have known him who is from the beginning. I write to you, **young men [and women]**, because you have overcome the evil one."* Let's look at these three types of people and how they can be prepared and trained to become spiritual parents within small groups and house churches.

Spiritual Babies

There are many spiritual babies (new Christians) in the church today, with few spiritual fathers and mothers available to disciple them. But the larger problem seems to be the many spiritual babies who have never grown up, many of them unaware they are still infants. Their spiritual chronological age may be 20, 30, 40, or 50 years old, but they remain on "the milk." They make a fuss when they don't get their own way, complain about not being fed, and have not yet taken spiritual responsibility to train the next generation.

Spiritual Young Men and Women

Spiritual young men and women, according to the Bible, have the Word of God abiding in them and have overcome the wicked one. They have learned to feed on the Word for themselves in order to overcome the devil. But they have not yet become spiritual fathers or mothers.

When I was a child, I thought my father knew everything. When I became an adolescent, I felt there were a few things he didn't know. By the time I was in my mid-teens, in my youthful arrogance, I just figured my father was still living in the stone ages. But when I became a father, I was amazed at how much my father had learned during the past few years! The truth was, in my becoming a father, my perspective changed. In the same way, having spiritual children also changes our perspective.

One of the greatest catalysts to maturity as a Christian is to become a spiritual father or mother. Many of the problems that surface in churches today are the product of: (1) spiritual young men and women who are full of the Word of God but have not had the experience of becoming spiritual parents, and (2) church leaders who have not released and encouraged the spiritual young men and women within their church to have their own spiritual children.

Spiritual Fathers and Mothers

So how does a young man or woman become a spiritual parent? He or she could quote the entire Book of Leviticus from memory and still not be a spiritual parent. Let's review what Paul said to the Corinthian church in First Corinthians 4:15-16.

Even though you have ten thousand guardians in Christ,
you do not have many fathers, for in Christ Jesus I became

your father through the gospel. Therefore I urge you to
imitate me.

The only way for a young man or woman to become a spiritual parent is to have children. We can have children either by adoption (becoming spiritual parents to those who already are believers but need to be discipled) or by natural birth (becoming spiritual parents to those we have personally led to Christ) and committing ourselves to helping them grow. The small group setting provides an ideal opportunity for everyone to experience a spiritual family and eventually become a spiritual parent themselves. The purpose of small group and house church multiplication is to see new spiritual parents take responsibility for a new spiritual family (a new small group or house church).

In the early 1970s, when LaVerne and I, with a team of young people, began to develop Paul-Timothy relationships with new Christians, I would meet with a few young men each week for Bible study, prayer, and to try to answer their questions about life. LaVerne did the same with young women. Watching them grow from spiritual babies, to young men and women, to spiritual parents has brought great joy to our lives. It has also caused great growth in our personal spiritual lives.

There is a tremendous need for spiritual parents in the church today. I can still hear the desperation in the voice of a dynamic young leader in New Zealand who opened his heart to me a few years ago. "I need a father. Where are the spiritual fathers today?" Jesus took 12 men and became a spiritual father to them for three and a half years. He knew that Christianity was caught more than taught. He ministered to the multitudes, but most of His time was spent with these few men. His disciples changed the world. By our Lord's example, we can do the same.

You Can Be a Spiritual Parent!

Perhaps you feel you have already tried to be a spiritual parent, but you feel you have failed. Trust God for grace to start again. Mother Teresa once said, "God does not demand that I be successful. God demands that I be faithful. When facing God, results are not important. Faithfulness is what is important."[2]

Maybe you never had a spiritual father or mother. You can give someone else something you never had by being his or her spiritual parent. You do not need to be perfect, just faithful and obedient. If you and I wait until we think we are ready to be the perfect parent, it will never happen. And remember, you may be a spiritual parent to someone for a short season of time or for many years; this is up to the Lord, not us.

Are you expecting the believers in your church, small group, or house church to become spiritual fathers or mothers? If not, you need to change your way of thinking. Many will become small group leaders, fulfilling their roles as spiritual parents in the coming days. And many small group leaders, currently experiencing "on-the-job training," will become future house church leaders, elders, church planters, and apostolic leaders. Remember, we train them to give them away!

Small group and house church leaders are called by the Lord to become spiritual parents to believers in small groups. Elders and pastors become spiritual parents to small-group leaders. Apostolic leaders become spiritual parents to elders and pastors. The Lord is restoring spiritual parenting to His Church today.

In the next chapter, we will discuss the importance of fitting into the Body of Christ and how God places us within spiritual families for just the right fit!

QUESTIONS TO THINK ABOUT
From Chapter 5

1. In your own words, explain how a spiritual father or mother can invest in someone's life.

2. Do you presently have a spiritual parent? Have you had a spiritual parent in the past? Explain.

3. Are you a spiritual parent to another person? Explain.

CHAPTER 6

Spiritual Families

The Lord sees His people much differently than we often perceive them. We believe He sees us, first of all, as individual believers, bought by the blood of Jesus. But He also sees His people within spiritual families. This is illustrated in the Old Testament when the Lord told Joshua there was sin in the camp. Notice how the Lord instructed Joshua to identify the man who was in sin. The Lord could have simply pointed him out to Joshua, but He didn't. Instead, Joshua had to go through tribes, clans, and families until he arrived at the guilty individual. There are levels of accountability in the Kingdom of God.

> *Early the next morning Joshua had Israel come forward by tribes, and Judah was taken. The clans of Judah came forward, and he took the Zerahites. He had the clan of the Zerahites come forward by families, and Zimri was taken. Joshua had his family come forward man by man, and*

Achan son of Carmi, the son of Zimri, the son of Zerah, of the tribe of Judah, was taken (Joshua 7:16-18).

All families have extended families. My immediate family lives with me in the same house. We spend a lot of time together. On occasion we spend time with our parents and brothers and sisters and their children. Once each year we spend time with some of our cousins and their children. I don't even know all of these people by name, but they are still a part of my family! By only meeting in congregations on Sunday mornings, the church of today is emphasizing the extended spiritual family rather than the immediate spiritual family (small groups and house churches with people we know well).

The question we need to ask is this: How can these spiritual families be most effective? Part of the answer to this question is to be found in recognizing that the Lord sees each of us as a part of various spiritual spheres.

First of all, He sees us as members of a natural family. In God's plan, families (spouses and children) are to function as little churches. Nearly everything the church does our family should do. In my own family, we teach, pray, and discuss our faith with those who have not yet been made spiritually alive through faith in Jesus. Sometimes we share communion together in our home. This is similar to how a small group should function. In fact, the church meeting as a small group is a type of spiritual family.

A clan is a group of families that are related. We have come to believe that clusters of small groups that relate closely together as a congregation or a house church network are a type of spiritual clan. The believers in the New Testament church who met from house to house in specific areas were a type of spiritual clan. They were simply an extended spiritual family. For example, according to Romans 16, the believers in Rome met together in homes. But it is also clear that they were in relationship to one another throughout the city.

The third sphere of relationships is that of a spiritual "tribe." For some, this refers to a denomination. For others, it may be a group of churches that work together as a network or as an apostolic fellowship with a common vision. For us, the DOVE Christian Fellowship International churches that partner together from various parts of the world represent a spiritual tribe.

The Israelite people consisted of 12 tribes and a multitude of clans and families. They were corporately known as the children of Israel. In the same way, the Lord sees His Church as being composed of believers in families, clans, and tribes who represent the whole of the Kingdom of God.

> *You are all sons of God through faith in Christ Jesus.... There is neither Jew nor Greek, slave nor free, male nor female, for you are all one in Christ Jesus* (Galatians 3:26,28).

The walls have been broken down! We need one another. I have noticed that when a particular group does not relate to other groups in the Body of Christ, in most cases they eventually feel a need to reach out beyond themselves for practical fellowship and accountability. We believe the Lord places this desire in our hearts. Each "tribe" has something to offer the other, expressions of the Church of Jesus Christ. We must work together. We need each other!

United We Stand

Unity is not created by no longer having denominations or spiritual tribes. Unity comes when believers and leaders of churches, denominations, and networks of churches and house churches can each obey the calling God has given them, while simultaneously affirming the vision God has given to others. Then, as they confirm, support, and pray for one another, the Lord will bless them with tremendous oneness.

It would be foolish for the U.S. Air Force, Marines, Army, Navy, and Coast Guard to dismantle their area of responsibility and expertise in order to achieve unity. Unity comes as each branch of the military fulfills its responsibilities while maintaining clear communication with the rest of the Armed Forces.

The same principle applies to the church. Let's pursue what the Lord has called us to do with all of our hearts and encourage those in other "spiritual tribes." Let's pray for one another and support each other any way we can. As we do so, Jesus will build His Church among us.

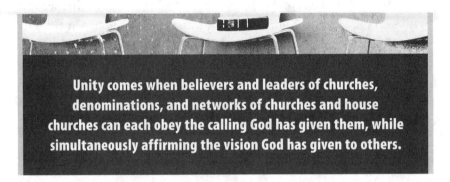

Unity comes when believers and leaders of churches, denominations, and networks of churches and house churches can each obey the calling God has given them, while simultaneously affirming the vision God has given to others.

I have the privilege of praying on a regular basis with spiritual leaders representing thousands of Christians in our area from different spiritual tribes (denominations). It is tremendous to pray with other servant-leaders in the Body of Christ. A while back, a group of pastors and other spiritual leaders took some time away to pray, fellowship, learn from one another, and play basketball at a local retreat center. The Lord gave us a tremendous sense of His presence as we spent this time together. The Lord is teaching His Church that there is no competition in His Kingdom.

When the Lord called Gideon to deliver the people of God, Gideon saw himself as an individual member of his family, clan, tribe, and of the Israelite extended family.

> *The Lord turned to him and said, "Go in the strength you have and save Israel out of Midian's hand. Am I not sending you?"*

"But Lord," Gideon asked, "how can I save Israel? My clan is the weakest in Manasseh, and I am the least in my family" (Judges 6:14-15).

When Jesus fed the 5,000, He saw more than a sea of faces. He saw individual people and knew that it was most practical for them to be placed in groups.

Then Jesus directed them to have all the people sit down in groups on the green grass. So they sat down in groups of hundreds and fifties (Mark 6:39-40).

We are convinced there is a God-ordained need within every man, woman, and child to belong to a small group of people with whom they can relate. In some cases, this need may be denied due to the hurt and pain of broken or strained past relationships; however, deep down, the need is still there.

As those who have God-given authority and responsibility for the local church, we have a choice. If we do not provide the new wineskins (small groups) the Lord ordains, the door will be open for the devil to form unhealthy groups. The counterfeit will be groups of people who are backbiting and complaining and spreading spiritual cancer throughout the Body or cults that employ the same principle in the service of a lie. Let's cooperate with the Lord and provide healthy small groups and house churches for God's people so they are not ensnared by the counterfeit.

Homogeneous Cells

In the same way that we have various kinds of living cells in our body, the church should be made up of various kinds of homogeneous small groups and house churches, each having a different target group.

According to the *New Merriam-Webster Dictionary*, *homogeneous* means "of the same or similar kind; of uniform makeup or structure."

Cells in your body have certain similarities, such as a nucleus, but they are all unique and different, depending on the work they do in the body. For example, all liver cells are in the same place—the liver. All heart cells are located in the heart. Each cell functions within the capacity and environment that God created for it.

With small groups and house churches, each serves the entire church or house church network in the way God has ordained in His sovereign wisdom. He places each person where He wants him or her to be, in order for him or her to learn and to serve others in a way that is most effective. The most common type of small groups and house churches in the DCFI family of churches usually consists of a mixed group with a balance of families, young and older people, and singles. These small groups of believers may have a mission of intercession, praying actively for people in their communities and the church. Others periodically serve at local rescue missions or serve the homeless. Still others may spend time ministering to lonely senior citizens at the nursing home.

There have been small groups and house churches that have reached out solely to the unchurched children in their communities. They are convinced that today's kids have vast spiritual needs and must be led into an early and deeply meaningful relationship with Jesus Christ before their tender hearts are hardened by the world. The children's small groups and house churches tailor their message for kids, and the groups are kept exciting and relevant and create in the children a desire to trust God.

Youth small groups have been tremendous! Young people who get involved in small-group leadership grow spiritually themselves as they reach out to others. When our daughter Katrina was 15 years old, she began to serve as an assistant small group leader in a youth cell that met in our home. It gave her the opportunity to grow in the Lord and develop leadership skills that will be with her for her entire life. Many times youth small groups are responsible to plan evangelistic outreaches or social events for the entire youth group in the church or local congregation.

One junior high small group outreach to skaters resulted in an ongoing Bible study for the skaters, along with an indoor skate park constructed for them.

Some small groups and house churches may relate only to businessmen. Their focus is to reach out to other businessmen who need to believe in Christ. In the nation of Barbados, a small group started with the desire of targeting local businesspersons. A business lunch small group began weekly and eventually added dozens of white-collar workers to their local church.

Still other homogeneous small groups may include only women or men or singles. One time a small group was formed by single women who were concerned for unwed mothers. The group initially decorated a box with the word LIFE (Living Instruments for Emmanuel) on it. At each meeting, the women would bring small, practical gifts for a baby and deposit them in the box. After a few weeks of praying, the Lord led a single mother to their group, and they spent prime prayer time interceding for her and her unborn child. When the child was born, they had a lot of items to give, along with their prayers and encouragement.

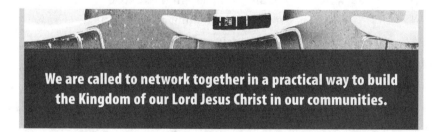

We are called to network together in a practical way to build the Kingdom of our Lord Jesus Christ in our communities.

In the same way that we need many kinds of cells in the human body to do the many tasks, so it is in the Body of Christ. While each of these small groups and house churches has its own vision, they need to flow with the vision of the entire local church (cluster of small groups) or house church network serving together to fulfill the Great Commission. No small group or house church is an island of its own. It is one part of a larger vision.

We are not just called to be a local church isolated from the rest of the Body of Christ. We are called of the Lord to be a part of a movement of the Holy Spirit. We are called to network together in a practical way to build the Kingdom of our Lord Jesus Christ in our communities. We are called to extend our hands to others around the world who have "caught the vision" to make disciples in every nation of the world.

How are disciples made? The next chapter explains how we first have to reach out in our communities and world by asking Jesus to lead us to those who have not yet determined to follow Him.

QUESTIONS TO THINK ABOUT
From Chapter 6

1. How does the Old Testament pattern for the nation of Israel (family, clan, tribe, etc.) compare to a church comprised of small groups?

2. Why is "structure" necessary in the Body of Christ? Contrast structure in the human body with structure in the church body.

3. Define how structure needs relationship and how relationship also needs structure.

CHAPTER 7

Reaching Out Beyond Ourselves

The primary focus of each small group and house church should be outreach and discipleship, rather than fellowship. Fellowship, then, will be a healthy by-product of the small group that is constantly reaching out to others.

There will be much prayer and interaction within the group to meet needs and form relationships, but the top priority must always be to bring in those who have not yet decided to believe in Christ. This causes the group to mature and multiply or reproduce another small group. It gives more believers the opportunity to use the gifts the Lord has given to them to reach pre-Christians and make disciples.

We are called to trust Him. The greatest catalyst that I know of to grow in Christ and to not be self-consumed is to get our eyes off of ourselves and instead look to Jesus and to the needs of those around us. A group of people who are always looking inward and are content to have the status quo will never grow and multiply. Looking inward prevents growth, like an ingrown toenail, and usually causes pain, competition, and stagnation.

When groups are content to stay the same, without knowing it, they build a wall around themselves, causing others to feel they are not welcome. The group having a heart to reach out to others is willing to change, enjoying wonderful fellowship in the process.

When I was newly married and a young missionary, I heard a man of God quote C.T. Studd, the famous missionary: "I do not wish to live 'neath sound of church or chapel bell; I want to run a rescue shop within a yard of hell." These words were life changing for me.

The main purpose for every small group and house church must be to run a rescue shop within a yard of hell. Otherwise, the group becomes a social club without any power. The Lord gives us power to be witnesses, not to sit around and enjoy nice, comfortable "bless-me" meetings.

> *But you will receive power when the Holy Spirit comes on you; and you will be My witnesses in Jerusalem, and in all Judea and Samaria, and to the ends of the earth* (Acts 1:8).

The church is not primarily a hospital; it is an army. Although armies do have medical units, they are for the purpose of getting the soldiers healed so they can get out on the battlefield and destroy the enemy. The focus is not the medical unit. The focus is on the battle and in winning the war. We are in a spiritual war! We do not have time to sit around and play church like children play war games. We need to rise up in faith and be the Church and destroy the works of darkness in Jesus' name!

When I was a young man, our nation was in the midst of the Vietnam War. Every year, Bob Hope would take an entourage to Vietnam to entertain the soldiers. Now let's face the facts. No one joined the army to go to Vietnam to see Bob Hope. They went to Vietnam to fight a war! However, while they were there they had the fringe benefit of being entertained by Bob Hope and his company.

Although the primary purpose of the small group and house church is to reach pre-Christians and disciple new believers, we also experience the fringe benefit of tremendous fellowship and relationships with people who care about us. They stand with us as we face hardships and struggles.

> **Although the primary purpose of the small group and house church is to reach pre-Christians and disciple new believers, we also experience the fringe benefit of tremendous fellowship and relationships with people who care about us.**

There will be many different creative approaches to reaching pre-Christians and making disciples as we work together in a small group or house church setting; however, the primary vision must be clear and fixed. We are called to fulfill the Great Commission. We don't necessarily fulfill the Great Commission by having an evangelistic teaching at every meeting or think that we must go out on the street to evangelize pre-Christians each week. The main focus of our vision must be to seek the Lord for ways to reach those who do not know Christ and make disciples.

One small group I was a part of printed up an attractive flyer with a big photo of our smiling group. One summer we canvassed our neighborhood by handing out the flyer to those who were newcomers to the community, along with a small house plant. We welcomed the new families to the neighborhood and invited them to our small group.

Some youth cells have used clowning as a regular outreach ministry for their group. Dressed as clowns, they go to parks, visit the elderly, and generally spread cheer and the Good News of Jesus wherever they go as they hand out balloons and do short skits.

Picnic evangelism is an informal way to reach family and friends with the message that God loves us and sent His Son so we can find forgiveness and new life through Him. Small group and house church members take the initiative to invite friends and relatives, who have not made a decision to follow Christ, to a picnic including free food, games, and entertainment. Sharing Christ at picnics is a big hit with some DOVE Kenya small groups in Nairobi; with its warm climate, picnics are possible throughout most of the year. Through the outreach of these family-oriented picnics, relationships are built and people come to faith in Christ.

When small groups and house churches have evangelism as an integral part of their focus, God often brings nonbelievers right into their group settings. Wendy befriended Susi, an atheist East German exchange student at her school. She invited Susi along to her small group, and over the next several months, Susi soaked in God's Word and asked many challenging questions of her new-found friends. It was an exciting day for the entire group when Susi announced she had made Jesus the Lord of her life and wanted to be baptized.

When individuals in small groups and house churches challenge each other to reach beyond themselves to make disciples, they will discover that God will give them many creative opportunities. Even if no one immediately comes to Christ through these opportunities, there is a spiritual dynamic released in the group that keeps our focus on the harvest fields instead of on ourselves. As we continue to sow, we will eventually reap.

The *Oikos* Principle

During the early 1980s, a group from our church took a trip to Seoul, Korea, to visit one of the largest churches in the world, Yoido Full Gospel Church. One of the principles that we learned during our time there was the "*oikos* principle."

What is an *oikos*? *Oikos* is the Greek word for household or house of people. Your *oikos* is that group of people with whom you relate on a regular basis. Every believer should apply the *oikos* principle to their lives as a way of infiltrating their spheres of influence with the Gospel of Jesus Christ.

Acts 10:2 speaks of Cornelius and all of his family (*oikos*). He and all his family were devout and God-fearing; he gave generously to those in need and prayed to God regularly.

> *...Cornelius was expecting them and had called together his relatives and close friends* [his oikos] (Acts 10:24).

Paul and Silas were in prison. In the midst of an earthquake the jailer became receptive to the Gospel. He invited his household to listen to Paul's message, and they were all made acceptable to God through faith in Christ. This group of people was his *oikos*.

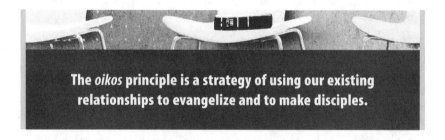

The *oikos* principle is a strategy of using our existing relationships to evangelize and to make disciples.

The *oikos* principle is a strategy of using our existing relationships to evangelize and to make disciples.

Groups of People Who Are a Part of Your *Oikos:*

- **Family and relatives.** Your Uncle Jack and Aunt Judy and cousin Ted are all part of your *oikos,* even if they live far away. If you maintain regular contact with them, they are part of your *oikos*.

- **Those who have common interests with you.** Those who play tennis with you are part of your *oikos*. Anyone you share a common interest with, such as an interest in computers, sewing, playing basketball, playing the guitar—these people are a part of your *oikos*.

- **Those who live in the same geographical location as you.** Your neighbors are a part of your *oikos*.

- **Those who have a common vocation.** Those whom you work with—your fellow employees—are a part of your *oikos*. If you are a construction worker, your *oikos* includes other construction workers. If you are a doctor, other professional people that you would relate with would be included in your *oikos*.

- **Others with whom you have regular contact.** These people may include your dentist, family doctor, mechanic, hairdresser, sales people, school officials, etc.

Those people in your *oikos* group will be much more receptive to the Gospel in God's timing because they trust you—you have built a relationship with them.

Sometimes Christians discover they have only other believers in their *oikos*. When this is the case, steps need to be taken to develop new circles of relationships. Some believers join soccer teams, neighborhood organizations, and other community groups to bring increase to their *oikos*.

More than 30 years ago, when my wife LaVerne and I and a group of young people began to play baseball, basketball, and other sports with youth in our local community, we built relationships with them and they became a part of our *oikos*. Because we established friendships with them on their turf, we could readily discuss the Good News of Jesus. Our *oikos* is part of God's strategy to reach the world.

One day, Jesus ministered to a man who was demon possessed. After he was delivered, the man begged Jesus for permission to follow Him. However, Jesus said:

> *"Return home and tell how much God has done for you."*
> *So the man went away and told all over town how much*
> *Jesus had done for him* (Luke 8:39).

Jesus sent him home to his *oikos*!

When Levi invited Jesus to his home for dinner, he invited his *oikos* members (see Luke 5:27-32). Zacchaeus had Jesus come to his home, and his whole household accepted Christ. This was his *oikos* (see Luke 19:9). Andrew asked Simon to come and get to know Jesus. Simon was Andrew's *oikos* member (see John 1:40-42). Philip asked Nathaniel to come and get to know Jesus. Nathaniel was Philip's *oikos* member (see John 1:44-45).

Small group and house church members have many everyday *oikos* opportunities. Ryan served as a small group leader at a DCFI church until he and his family moved to another state where they continued to be involved in small group ministry. Ryan relates this story from a few years back. He was at the drive-in movies when God used him:

> "It was just another Saturday night when my wife and I took my young cousin to a Disney movie at the drive-in," said Ryan. "We parked our very used Toyota with Jesus stickers plastered all over the back window, and I stepped out of the car to go to the snack bar. A guy named Jon stopped me and asked if I was a Christian, and then proceeded to tell me his story of a life lived in disobedience to God. I told him how Jesus changed my life and that before I knew God, I was hurting and longing for real purpose. I explained how I had tried to find fulfillment in sports and later had joined the U.S. Marine Corps in hopes that being successful there would bring me a sense of accomplishment. That night, Jon knelt right beside

that snack bar at the drive-in and made Jesus the Lord of his life.

"The next week my wife and I, with my little cousin, returned to the drive-in and parked the car. This time, before I could even get out of the car, a woman I had never seen before came to the car and asked if I was the person who had prayed with Jon. She asked me to come to her car to meet Jon's mom (notice the expanding *oikos!*). This precious lady, who had been an alcoholic for years, asked Jesus into her life that night and was set free!"

Bob's story is another one that illustrates how an entire family *oikos* was impacted with the Good News of Christ. After Bob and his wife found new life and stability in Christ, Bob was burdened for his parents, brothers, and sisters who were far from God. Bob, along with his home group, prayed that God would allow him to contact his father, with whom the family had lost touch. Although the situation seemed hopeless, through a series of miracles Bob reached his dad, along with other family members on a trip that crisscrossed the United States. His dad was living with Bob's half-sister, and they both received Jesus into their lives. Bob and his sister traveled to another state to explain the message of the hope Jesus offers with her brother, and he and his wife made a decision to follow Christ. Continuing on to yet another state, Bob contacted his mother, and she responded immediately, "I want to accept Jesus." It helped that Bob's oldest brother had accepted the Lord a few days earlier. Looking back on it, Bob is sure that the Spirit of God moved so freely in response to the many prayers of the believers praying for Bob's "miracle missionary outreach" to his family *oikos.*

The *oikos* strategy is the most natural way of fulfilling the Great Commission. Nearly every Christian has at least 20 people in his or her *oikos.* These 20 people plus their *oikos* gives the potential of 400 contacts (20x20). People want the Truth! They are waiting for real Christians whom they can trust to give them the Truth (Jesus).

You may want to write a list of people in your *oikos*. Pray and ask God to show you two or three of the people whom you're most concerned about and begin to pray for these people and reach out to them. If they are pre-Christians, you will be involved in evangelism. If they are struggling in their Christian lives, God may call you to be involved in discipleship. Either way, you are called to pray for them.

One time a small group leader in one of the DCFI churches received a phone call from someone in his group. "Do you have any holy water?" he was asked. The small group leader did not grow up in a Roman Catholic tradition and was not expecting this type of request; however, he wanted to meet this woman where she was at, so he asked her for further details.

She explained her concern for her daughter and her boyfriend. Strange things were happening in their home. An object had jumped off the stove, and other unexplainable supernatural things were happening in their house. "Could I come over to your daughter and her boyfriend's home to pray?" he asked her.

"Oh yes!" she exclaimed. "And I want to be there when you come." The small group leader and his wife went over to their home to pray. After a time of sharing the Word of God, the young man received Jesus Christ as Lord. His girlfriend also expressed a desire to obey the Lord, and they were married a short time later. They started serving in a small group and were discipled and trained to lead others to Jesus.

Another small group leader discussed his faith in Christ with a salesman who came into his place of business. Later the salesman received the Lord and got involved with believers in a group in his local area. The small group began to pray for the salesman's mother, who had not yet accepted Christ. She received the Lord a few weeks before she passed away. Small groups and house churches that understand the *oikos* principle do not have a hard time focusing their attention on those who do not yet follow Christ. It becomes a very natural way to fulfill the Great Commission.

Some small groups and house churches use the Alpha Course, a 10-week course that explores some of the basic truths of the Christian faith. Alpha originated at an Anglican church, Holy Trinity Brompton, in

London in the 1970s and is used widely across all denominations as a way to invite friends who are not believers in Christ to learn the basics of the Bible. Other small groups and house churches ask the Lord to lead them to a man or woman of peace in their community whose heart is being prepared by the Holy Spirit to give their life to Christ (see Luke 10). These men or women of peace are people of influence, who when they give their lives to Christ, influence many others within their *oikos* also to give their lives to Christ.

Show Hospitality

Our homes are centers for ministry. In both house church and small group settings, homes often are the places where "pre-Christians" feel most comfortable. They can see that we are real people as we sit around the table eating ice cream or playing games. Being open and friendly as we share the things the Lord has given us creates an atmosphere where people feel relaxed; we can readily share the love of Jesus in personal and practical ways. The Bible gives this important advice on sharing what we have:

> *Offer hospitality to one another without grumbling. Each one should use whatever gift he has received to serve others, faithfully administering God's grace in its various forms* (1 Peter 4:9-10).

"Hospitality" is cheerfully sharing food, shelter, or spiritual refreshment to those whom God brings into your life. It is using your home and the material things God has given you as a means to serve others and build relationships. And it's fun!

There is a difference between entertaining and showing hospitality. Entertaining often emphasizes having a nice "party" or meal, while hospitality focuses on the needs of those who have come into our homes. When serving through hospitality, we should not hesitate to invite people to our home because of a lack of sumptuous or prepared food. Why not keep a few snacks or cans of soup on hand just in case? The truth is—hospitality doesn't always have to include food.

We should not be anxious about a little dirt or dust. A genuine, warm welcome will bless people a whole lot more than sweeping the floor before they come. We should be much more concerned about fellowship than about our home being spotless or having an elaborate meal. All too often, concentrating too much on elegance can actually become a hindrance to fellowship. Some of the best times of hospitality are those times when a plate of fruit, hot dogs, ice cream, or canned soup is shared as people get to know one another.

Jesus reprimanded Martha, after He came into her home, for being so overwhelmed with all her preparations. She became more concerned about serving than about the One she served. Mary, on the other hand, sought the important thing—fellowship with her Guest (see Luke 10:38-42).

If God has given you the grace to serve big meals when people come to your home and you love doing it—that's great. If you become anxious, like Martha, it is a warning light for you to reevaluate. Remember, it's not the food that's important but the fellowship! The Holy Spirit builds relationships as we spend time with people in our *oikos*.

Invite Those Who Cannot Invite You Back

Then Jesus said to His host:

> *When you give a luncheon or dinner, do not invite your friends, your brothers or relatives, or your rich neighbors; if you do, they may invite you back and so you will be repaid. But when you give a banquet, invite the poor, the crippled, the lame, the blind, and you will be blessed. Although they cannot repay you, you will be repaid at the resurrection of the righteous* (Luke 14:12-14).

God is especially honored when we invite those into our homes who cannot invite us back. A young man told a small group leader, "The first time I came into your home, I sensed the presence of God." Another told him, "The reason people love to come into your home is because they sense the peace of God." We must realize that the Lord's presence is in our homes. Expect people to sense the presence of the Lord in your home.

Open the door of your home to those who have needs. Romans 12:13 tells us to share with God's people who are in need and to practice hospitality. God is calling us to practical hospitality, expecting nothing in return. It is a commandment, not an option.

Practical Suggestions for Hospitality

When Hospitality Includes a Meal:

- Keep food on hand that can be made quickly.

- If married, the spouse should help prepare and clean up afterward.

- Singles, if your parents or roommates are uncomfortable with your inviting friends to your home when they are present, use your home when they are away, or go to a restaurant.

- Pray with people in your home. A great time to start is before mealtime. (Remember, those who were walking on the road to Emmaus had their spiritual eyes opened as Jesus blessed the food.)

Other Suggestions for Hospitality:

- Help guests to relax. Give them a drink or a snack so they have something to hold in their hands to keep them from feeling uncomfortable. If they are pre-Christians or Christians and smoke, be willing to provide an ashtray.

- Be open to the leading of the Holy Spirit to pray for or with them.

- Use tools such as tracts, books, CDs, DVDs, music, pictures, and wall plaques to help you in discussing spiritual things. The booklet entitled *What Does it Mean to Be a Real Christian?* [1] is an excellent tool to use to lead someone into a personal relationship with Jesus.

Called to the Nations

Another way that small groups and house churches can reach out beyond themselves is by adopting a missionary or a church leader from a church in another part of the world. We sometimes call this "embracing our missionaries."[2] Jesus instructed us to remember that His house is a *"house of prayer for all nations"* (Mark 11:17). The Lord's heart is in missions. Each small group and house church needs to have its heart in the same place—in the mission fields of the world.

Small groups and house churches that embrace a missionary or a church leader or church in another part of the world will send notes of encouragement to the missionary or foreign church leader. If they are embracing a missionary, they will pray for the missionary and become a practical link between the missionary and the local church. When the missionary comes home on furlough, the small group helps to serve the missionary in practical ways: housing, meals, travel, and fellowship. One small group that I am aware of has sent a former member to a foreign nation. This group will stay extra late at times in order to use their Internet phone to call their former small group member who is in a time zone that is eight hours ahead. Even though it's 6:00 A.M. in his nation, he anxiously anticipates these times of communication and encouragement.

We encourage small groups and house churches to adopt a church leader from another nation. Since DCFI has a mandate from the Lord to be involved in church planting in the nations of the world, members have the opportunity to reach out to believers in other nations who are a part of the same "spiritual family." The Lord has built beautiful relationships between believers in various nations of the world who are involved in these "partner churches."

Each of our international churches in the continents of the world has a vision to multiply and send out laborers to the nations. We believe that new wineskins must be formed in the nations of the world to contain and train new believers during the spiritual awakening that the Lord is sending on the earth! I have been so encouraged when spending time with the believers in DOVE Kenya and hearing their vision to reach the nations in the continent of Africa and beyond with the Good News of Jesus. They are already involved in planting churches in Uganda, Rwanda, and India. Sitting with the DOVE Scotland leadership and hearing them talk about the vision the Lord has given them to see churches birthed from outside of their nation has been thrilling. And believers in DOVE Christian Fellowship-New Zealand, Canada, Bulgaria, the Netherlands, the Caribbean, and Latin America now have a vision for church planting in nations outside of their own.

Those who lead these international churches are national leaders whom the Lord has raised up during the past few years. It's a joy to work with these Christian leaders as we labor together in preparing "new wineskins" to preserve the harvest that the Lord is bringing into His Kingdom.

Reaching International Students

One area where small groups and house churches can have a great impact on world missions is in international student ministry. To date, some 500,000 international students study in the United States. This is roughly three-fourths of the entire international student population worldwide. They generally comprise the academic top 5 to 10 percent of their young people, and many come from nations closed to traditional Western missionary activity. Furthermore, many universities are now actively recruiting internationals to come and study at their institutions, all the way from top Ivy League schools to community colleges.

This is a tremendous opportunity for hospitality evangelism. When Paul laid out the qualifications for elders to Titus, he mentioned "hospitality" as one of the required characteristics (Titus 1:8). The Greek word used here for hospitality is *philoxenos,* "to love the foreigner." It is interesting to note that Paul defines hospitality as that which we do for strangers, not our friends and families.

Through holiday picnics, weekend and semester break housing, recreational activities, and invitations to celebrate our religious holidays with us, small groups and house churches can build a circle of friends that can reach the international student with the Good News of Jesus Christ. According to surveys, the one thing international students who are living in America want most after an American degree is an American friend. Reaching them at this crucial time when they are confronted with relativism and secularism on their campuses can make an impact not only on their own lives, but perhaps even the destiny of a nation.

For most internationals, their North American degrees will be tickets to positions of relative influence and power in their nations. Sharing the Good News about Jesus with them can have a rippling effect far beyond their own personal lives. Their contact with Christianity could cause them to look with favor on missions efforts in their own countries and the national churches there. They will most likely have significant influence in their professional sphere and could even receive a call from the Lord to evangelize their own nation. All it takes is a willingness to give of our time and love, a determination to overcome social and cultural barriers, and the boldness to share the Good News of Jesus with the international student when the time is appropriate.[3]

God has called us to use the small groups and house churches as new vessels for the harvest. They are tools for making disciples, beginning in our local area and then reaching out to the nations. Every ministry within DCFI assists in the building of these "underground churches"— the small groups and house churches. For example, one of the purposes of our mission ministry, DOVE Mission International, is to help every believer in every small group and house church experience the blessing of teaming with others to reach the nations. Our publication company provides resources for small group and house church ministry.

An exciting, modern-day example of an underground church experiencing a great revival and making many new disciples took place in Ethiopia. In 1982 half of all the evangelical churches in Ethiopia were closed due to harassment, legal banning, and persecution. The Meserete Kristos Church fell under a complete ban. All of their church buildings were seized and used for other purposes. Several of their prominent leaders were imprisoned for years without trial or accusation.

The church membership at that time was approximately 5,000 believers. The fires of persecution got hotter and hotter each year, forcing them to go underground and meet in clandestine home groups. Nearly a decade later, the Marxist government fell. The same government leaders who closed the doors of the church buildings a few years before led the procession of God's people back into the buildings. However, the Church had grown "underground" from 5,000 to over 50,000 people!

During persecution, these believers met from house to house in small groups. Hundreds of believers began to get involved in the work of ministry in these groups. They no longer were focusing on the church building or the programs of the church. Their time together was spent in prayer, reaching those who have not yet determined to follow Christ, and making disciples.

In my study of church history, over and over again before any great move of the Holy Spirit, there were small groups of dedicated people who prayed and searched the Scriptures. The great revivals and outpourings of the Holy Spirit are usually traced to these seemingly insignificant gatherings of a few fervent intercessors.

Is it going to take persecution for us to experience this same kind of revival? Focusing on Jesus and the church meeting in small groups and house churches takes our emphasis off of meetings and programs. We can focus on Jesus and on the Great Commission. Is it possible that sometimes we are so busy going to church meetings that we do not have time to be true Christ followers and examples to the unevangelized? Small groups and house churches provide the atmosphere for believers to learn practical Christian living in an everyday setting.

In the next chapters we will look at leadership within small groups. How should a person lead? Jesus modeled for us how we should conduct ourselves. He took on the role of a servant and led through serving those around Him. That is the mark of a true leader.

QUESTIONS TO THINK ABOUT
From Chapter 7

1. Explain how "outreach" should be the primary focus of a small group or house church.

2. If a small group or house church loses sight of outreach, what then is the natural tendency of that group?

3. Make a list of persons that you presently have in your *oikos*. Prayerfully choose two or three of them to focus on for this next season of time.

PART

II

GRASSROOTS LEADERSHIP
DEVELOPMENT

CHAPTER 8

Leading Through Servanthood

*Your attitude should be the same as that of Christ Jesus:
Who, being in very nature God, did not consider equality
with God something to be grasped, but made Himself
nothing, taking the very nature of a servant...* (Philippians
2:5-7).

Leadership Means Servanthood

Jesus is our role model for leadership. He was and is the greatest leader
who ever lived. He led by being a servant to all of those around Him. He
knew who He was because of His intimate relationship with His Father,
and out of that relationship He ministered to the needs of individuals.

In the same way, true leaders whom God is using mightily today have
these few things in common: they have an intimate relationship with the

Father; they know how to pray; they are humble; they are totally dependent on Jesus; and they are servants. If you would observe them when they are not in the spotlight, you would find them serving others.

As a young pastor, I was in Ohio at a leadership meeting and was able to observe a well-known servant of the Lord behind the scenes. He was the kind of person who took every opportunity to notice those around him and was sensitive to their needs. As I watched one day, this man of God led a busboy to the Lord. Then he went out of his way to help this young man find a local church to attend the following weekend. This particular leader served wherever he found an opportunity. His life had a profound impact upon my life. He was a true servant-leader.

Leaders and servants are synonymous in the Body of Christ. When DCFI started, we never used the term "leader" in isolation. We were careful to call our leaders "servant-leaders," which implies true leadership, fashioned after Christ, based on serving others.

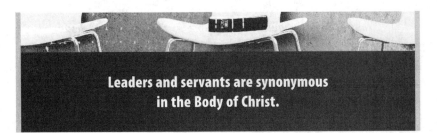

Leaders and servants are synonymous in the Body of Christ.

There is a saying, "Your life is speaking so loudly that I cannot hear the words you are saying." Telling others to serve when we're not serving is like a parent telling a child not to smoke, while puffing on a cigarette. When people see that their leaders do not give in to the self-serving spirit of our age but instead serve and lift each other up, they will be encouraged to do likewise.

There are countless ways we may serve others. We can't serve everyone in the world. We can't meet all the needs; but we are called to a small group or house church, and we can start there. Set the standard. Be the example. Help someone move, serve a meal, visit a shut-in, or pray with someone who has a need. There are hundreds of examples I could give of the servanthood that takes place within small groups and house churches.

One group I know of gave time and money so a single mom, worn out by the demands of her young children, could take a vacation. Others have given time freely to help remodel or repaint a room in a member's house or to repair a car. When a small group member came to a meeting one day and announced that her toilet had just broken apart with water gushing everywhere, the leader immediately left the meeting to assist the woman's husband in buying and installing a new toilet. When a leader sets the example, soon others will be doing the same, and the Body of Christ will experience serving as a lifestyle.

A servant leader does not rule over people but rather supports them and lifts them up to God. In the world's system, leaders are expected to dominate those under them, but God has called us to follow the example of His Son, Jesus, and be a servant. By His example, Jesus made it clear that leaders are called to serve.

Jesus Taught His Disciples Servanthood

> *Jesus called them together and said, "You know that the rulers of the Gentiles lord it over them, and their high officials exercise authority over them. Not so with you. Instead, whoever wants to become great among you must be your servant, and whoever wants to be first must be your slave— just as the Son of Man did not come to be served, but to serve, and to give His life as a ransom for many"* (Matthew 20:25-28).

When the mother of James and John came to Jesus and asked if her sons could sit on the right and left hand of His throne in His Kingdom, Jesus told her, "You do not know what you ask." When the other ten disciples heard about it, they were angry, jealous, and resentful. Jesus responded with these words, "Whoever desires to become a leader must become a slave." He did not say that it is wrong to be great, or wrong to be a leader; but greatness according to the world system is totally different than greatness from Jesus' perspective.

In John 13 we read that Jesus sent His disciples to prepare the Passover. When Jesus arrived, He realized that there was a problem. The disciples were arguing about who should wash their feet. Since there was no servant present, and it was customary for a servant to wash the feet of the family and guests as they came in from the dusty streets, the disciples were frustrated.

Without a word, Jesus took a towel and wrapped it around Himself. He knelt down and began to wash the disciples' feet. It was too much for Peter to handle. He balked at the idea that Jesus was willing to do the job of a lowly servant. Like Peter, we are sometimes proud and reluctant to be served. Other times, we must strip away our selfishness in order to serve others. In a small group or house church setting, we learn how to serve and to be served.

Leadership Without Servanthood

Rehoboam became king of Israel after Solomon died. He consulted two groups of counselors for wisdom to govern God's people properly. The older group, who had served before his father, Solomon, spoke these words, *"If you will be kind to these people and please them and give them a favorable answer, they will always be your servants"* (2 Chron. 10:7).

Then Rehoboam went to the younger group who told him to tell the people, "If you thought you had a heavy yoke to bear under my father, just wait. I will be much tougher!" Rehoboam listened to the advice of the young men and lost 10 of the 12 tribes of Israel because he didn't obey the biblical principle of serving.

God says that if we serve others and are kind to them, then they will also desire to serve us. Our true motive must be to serve others because Jesus Christ served us unselfishly on the cross 2,000 years ago. As we serve out of a pure heart, our sowing in servanthood will allow us to reap the benefits.

Sowing and Reaping Servanthood

An important key to your success as a leader is for you to serve in the small group or house church setting in which the Lord has placed you. Ask yourself the question, "How can I best serve this group?"

The greatest training for leadership is to be willing to serve, and then to do whatever needs to be done. Be practical. Find something that needs to be done and do it. Greet people at the door, pick up someone who needs a ride, take a meal, clean someone's home, help a family move, or fix a car.

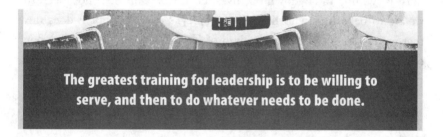

The greatest training for leadership is to be willing to serve, and then to do whatever needs to be done.

As a leader, you are an example to those in your group, so you need to be setting the standard for servanthood. Like Paul, the apostle, you need to be able to say to those in your group, *"Follow my example, as I follow the example of Christ"* (1 Cor. 11:1).

As you set the example, others will follow. For instance, if you are in a cell-based church, when you serve in some capacity at the Sunday morning congregational meetings, such as car parking, ushering, or children's ministry, those in your small group will be challenged to do the same.

Realize that serving others takes time. As a true servant, take all the time that is necessary to serve others in order to build good, trusting relationships. When you spend time with people in social contacts, or do things with others that are just fun or helpful, you are planting the seeds of friendship that will produce a harvest for God's Kingdom.

How do you respond to a phone call at 2:00 A.M.? You need to respond with the heart of a servant! It may take some practice, but a servant will answer, "Hello! What can I do for you?" Rather than, "Man! Do you know what time it is?" Untimely phone calls can tell us what we are really made of!

If we get upset, we are like a snake rising up, ready to strike out and demand our rights, as we respond out of a wrong spirit. The serpent in the Garden of Eden was only concerned about himself and his "rights." Actually, we don't have any rights because we've laid them down at the foot of the cross. The Lord gives us privileges and responsibilities.

Jesus gave up His rights as God and went to the cross as a lamb goes to the slaughter. As Jesus laid down His rights as the Lamb of God, we must be willing to lay down our lives for others. This does not mean that we are to be wimps who live with a martyr's complex, but it does mean that we can be so secure as children of God that we will gladly lay down our rights and expectations to help others to be strengthened in Christ. (See Philippians 2:1-16.)

If a neighbor's house is on fire, how do you respond? Do you say, "I hope that big fire truck doesn't drive on my lawn!" or "I hope I don't get smoke in my house"?

No, I'm sure you would say, "I'll do whatever I can to serve my neighbors while they're in this crisis."

If someone in our small group or house church has a problem, how should we respond? By doing all we can to serve and take care of the problem. Not because it's a big hassle for us and we want to get it over with, but because we want to see this person built strong in Christ. It's not only our actions that are important, but our attitude as well. *Lord, teach us to have the heart of a servant.*

Hirelings or Shepherds

"I'm sick and tired of people walking all over me." "Everyone is taking advantage of me." "No one appreciates what I'm doing." Those thoughts may cross the mind of every leader sooner or later because servanthood often requires perseverance, and it's not all fun. But if this becomes our attitude, we'll never make it as a servant leader. Remember, we must give up our rights. We take our selfish rights to the cross of Jesus. Then there will be nothing left to hurt us. Paul said, *"I die every day"* (1 Cor. 15:31).

If we do not act like servants, the Bible calls us "hirelings." A hireling gets paid to tend the sheep, but when the wolves come, the hireling runs away and leaves the sheep defenseless.

> *But a hireling, he who is not the shepherd, one who does not own the sheep, sees the wolf coming and leaves the sheep and flees; and the wolf catches the sheep and scatters them. The hireling flees because he is a hireling and does not care about the sheep* (John 10:12-13 NKJV).

Hirelings have no personal love for the sheep, no investment of the heart. The Scriptures tell us:

> *The goal of this command is love, which comes from a pure heart and a good conscience and a sincere faith...* (1 Timothy 1:5).

> *Dear children, let us not love with words or tongue but with actions and in truth* (1 John 3:18).

Hireling leaders of small groups or house churches are those tending sheep with the wrong motivation. They are not true shepherds. Their motivation is only for personal gain and personal pride.

Shepherds are servant leaders who are willing to lay aside their own agendas in order to serve others. There are, of course, times when it is proper for a servant leader to say "no." Even Jesus left the multitudes and withdrew into the wilderness to pray and be refreshed.

We do need boundaries in our relationships. If we are giving and giving to others or filling an excessive amount of their needs, always saying "yes" rather than saying "no," we actually hurt the relationships, hindering people from growing and developing on their own. Ask the Holy Spirit to help identify where healthy boundaries will grow relationships rather than limit them. Obviously, our motivation needs to be that the Holy Spirit is leading us to say "no," not just because we are tired of serving.

The Motivation of a Servant Leader

One day, soon after I was married, I decided to surprise my wife and wash the dishes for her while she was out. I scrubbed the dishes spotless and expected a big thanks from LaVerne when she returned. When she didn't even notice, I had to practically gag myself with my dishcloth to keep from blurting out, "Don't you see what a great job I've done?" I hadn't learned to be a servant. I served for praise, instead of serving because I had the heart of a servant.

The number one motivation of a servant leader is to love God and serve His people out of a heart of love. If our only motivation is to have a good, prosperous, wonderful small group or house church—it is wrong. Our first motivation must be to love Jesus, love His people, and desire to reach those who do not yet believe in Christ. When we do that, the natural result will be a good, healthy, exciting group.

Your motivation as a leader probably will be tested at times. God may bring people into your life who are hard for you to love. Jesus said:

> ...*whatever you did for one of the least of these brothers of Mine, you did for Me*... (Matthew 25:40).

One night a young man in a backslidden state stopped by our home. He had been drinking and vomited all over himself and the driveway in front of our home. We took him into our home, loved him, and helped him to get cleaned up. God had given us an opportunity to practice the principles of the Kingdom of God with proper motivation.

Jesus loved the people He served.

> *When He saw the crowds, He had compassion on them, because they were harassed and helpless, like sheep without a shepherd* (Matthew 9:36).

Again, a small group or house church leader's motivation must be that he is moved with compassion. If we don't feel compassion, we must ask God to give it to us. Once we have the mind of Christ, we will eagerly seek those scattered sheep in order to help them.

Sometimes the Lord brings a "brother or sister sandpaper" into our lives. Something about them rubs us the wrong way. The Lord is putting us to the test. If we do not learn the lesson, the Lord will probably bring someone else into our lives who may be even tougher to handle. Welcome to the real world!

The small group and house church setting can give believers the secure atmosphere they need to become mature in the Body of Christ. In small groups and house churches we are being knit together with other people whom we are learning to love as Jesus does, and our Lord continues His good work of building His character in us.

Serving Through Building Relationships

> *From Him the whole body, joined and held together by every supporting ligament, grows and builds itself up in love, as each part does its work* (Ephesians 4:16).

We believe that the "ligaments" the Bible is speaking about refer to relationships in the Body of Christ. Small group and house church meetings are only tools that God uses to build relationships. If a small group leader is not a servant, he gets uptight when people do not come to meetings. If, however, he is a true servant leader, he will always be building relationships with people outside of his group; and they will "beat the doors down" to come to the meetings because they know he cares for them. People recognize sincere servanthood. Children gather at mealtime around their mother and father because they are family. They know that they are loved and their parents care for them. They want to be together.

Some potential small group leaders and house church leaders have a "preacher's itch." They are more concerned about speaking to others than they are about serving others. It is very noble to want to proclaim God's message to the world; however, our motivation must be to love people. We cannot be motivated by selfish gain or recognition. If we have the heart of a servant, people will come because God builds His Church on loving relationships.

Dwight L. Moody was the Billy Graham of a century ago. He had 1,200 young people in his Sunday school class in Chicago. Many wanted to help him teach. He knew that only servants would have successful classes, so he allowed the young people to go to any class that they wanted. Those teachers who had true servants' hearts and were willing to build relationships with these young people had students in their classes. The others did not. This was Moody's screening process for small group leaders.

Serving Through Encouragement

But encourage one another daily, as long as it is called Today, so that none of you may be hardened by sin's deceitfulness (Hebrews 3:13).

Everyone gets discouraged at times. Everyone needs a friend who truly cares, who will listen and be understanding. As a small group or house church leader, you may not be able to personally encourage everybody daily. But you can be a catalyst in helping relationships develop. That way everyone in your group will be encouraged regularly.

A catalyst is an outside substance that speeds up a chemical reaction. In fresh, wet concrete, the calcium is the catalyst that causes it to harden quickly.

For example, as new Christians come into your group, you can pray about which individuals in your group are ready to disciple the new believers. If you sense God telling you that Ross could disciple Tom, a new believer, ask Ross to go along with you and Tom to breakfast or invite both Ross and Tom to your home to see if God would place them together in a relationship. You can be a catalyst in bringing a potential discipleship relationship together, but the Holy Spirit has to do the bonding. It is our job to pray, encourage, and allow God to bring people together because we cannot force relationships to happen.

It is especially important that you encourage a new Christian often. He needs daily contact and encouragement for at least a month after he makes a decision to follow Christ and regular contact for six months to a year. He is a spiritual baby and needs his spiritual "diapers" changed. If a new Christian tells you, "I'm discouraged. I don't know if it is worth the hassle of living for the Lord," as a true servant, you will pray with him and spend time encouraging him. Then the spiritual baby will say, "I feel much better. Thanks!" It's just a part of helping new Christians grow.

A new tree is very small, weak, and spindly when it's first planted, but it grows larger and stronger. When the roots are grounded, it no longer needs a stake to keep the wind from blowing it over. The same principle applies to new Christians. They need lots of support during their first weeks and months as a Christian.

The greatest ways we can serve the Body of Christ are through prayer and giving regular encouragement. Our responsibility is not to hear from God for other people, but rather, we are called to pray for them so that they can hear God's voice for themselves. We train and build them up by holding them up before God's throne in prayer and by modeling for them our dependency on the Word of God. We can be a godly example to them and discuss appropriate Scriptures with them.

As we care for them and love them, they will soon be built up to hear from God for themselves about decisions that they need to make in their daily lives. The Word of God says:

> But solid food belongs to those who are of full age, that is, those who by reason of use have their senses exercised to discern both good and evil (Hebrews 5:14).

Serving Those Who Are No Longer Active in Our Group

> Suppose one of you has a hundred sheep and loses one of them. Does he not leave the ninety-nine in the open country and go after the lost sheep until he finds it? (Luke 15:4).

Jesus' first priority was to go after the sheep that left the fold. We need to do the same. When people leave the fellowship that they had with other believers, the enemy is not just sitting nonchalantly in the corner. He is pursuing them.

We are all needy at times. Often when a member is depressed or has sinned and is pressed down with guilt (when he most needs encouragement), he avoids fellow Christians. A small group or house church needs to be a group of believers that is looking out for one another through the unpredictable turns of life. What should we do when someone is no longer active in the group?

It is important that we do not draw conclusions prematurely. Visit the person or give him a phone call or text him. People know when we sincerely care. Find out why he is not coming to the group. Maybe the Lord is calling him to another part of the Body of Christ, or maybe he is discouraged. A sheep that is sick needs attention. He may not respond immediately. Give him time for the Spirit of God to work in his life. But don't forget about him or think, "Oh well, he obviously wasn't committed anyway." If he is open to it, pray with him and encourage him to return (unless God is calling him to another place).

During the early days of DCFI, we discouraged people from changing from one small group to another, other than when the group multiplied. But we learned through experience that for the health of the small group, it was more important that each person was assured that the Lord had placed him in the group he attended. Sometimes people do not seem to fit into certain small groups of believers. For example, perhaps Tammy and Ray discover they are not comfortable in the group they started attending. They have little in common with the others in the group and have trouble relating. In these cases we encourage Tammy and Ray to visit some other small groups or house churches until they find their niche. When Tammy and Ray are candid with their small group leader or house church leader about their struggle to fit in, he can help them find the best place for them.

A small group or house church leader should never feel insecure when people leave the group to find another, but rather he should confirm his love and acceptance of the person who struggles to fit in. A small group or house church leader knows that people are like pieces to a puzzle. Some pieces fit together and others do not. When God's people are fit together properly by the Holy Spirit, they will experience the Lord's peace.

The Elijah Training Principle

Elijah the prophet lived out a spiritual principle that the Lord requires small group leaders, house church leaders, pastors, and other Christian leaders to live out in this generation. After suffering from deep depression, Elijah heard his God speak through a still, small voice. The Lord instructed him to recruit Elisha as an "apprentice" and train him to take his place (see 1 Kings 19:11-16). When Elisha asked Elijah for a double portion of his spirit, Elijah gave him clear instructions to receive this "double anointing." After Elijah's departure, Elisha performed twice as many miracles as Elijah.

My prayer for those I am responsible to disciple and train is that they may be used of God in a much greater way than I have been used. Jesus told His disciples that those who trusted in Him would do the works He does and even greater works (see John 14:12). And John the Baptist, a type of New Testament Elijah, stated clearly, *"He must become greater; I must become less"* (John 3:30). John's whole life was consumed with preparing the way for Jesus. The Lord has called us as small group and house church leaders, pastors, and Christian leaders to do the same—to see Jesus and others increase as we decrease. This must be our motivation. We are preparing servant leaders for the next generation.

In the next chapters we will take an in-depth look at the biblical qualifications and responsibilities of a small group and house church leader.

QUESTIONS TO THINK ABOUT
From Chapter 8

1. What must be the heart motive of true spiritual leaders?

2. What is the difference between a servant (shepherd) and a hireling?

3. Give an example of serving through building relationships and serving through encouraging others.

CHAPTER 9

Am I Qualified to Be a Leader?

We are all called to go, teach, and disciple the nations, but how can anyone be sure he is specifically called to lead a small group or house church? If the Lord has put the idea into your heart to lead a group, a good place to start is with this attitude, "Lord, I'm willing to begin by serving a few people, by loving and undergirding them as they fulfill what You have called them to do." If God desires to give you leadership responsibilities, He'll give you peace, faith, and often anticipation about it in your spirit.

God's basic method of choosing leaders in the Bible was seldom democratic (by popular vote). It was theocratic (by God Himself). When the Lord calls you, you know it in your heart. When God is calling you, the spiritual leadership and the people the Lord has placed around you will also sense the call of God on your life and confirm it. The Book of Proverbs tells us that a man's gift makes room for him. Although the literal translation of this Scripture speaks of a bribe, an important spiritual principle is implied. When God gives us a gift for a particular task, the people around us will acknowledge that gift and make room for it. It takes time, though, for that to happen:

> *They must first be tested; and then if there is nothing against them, let them serve as deacons* (1 Timothy 3:10).

> *But in fact God has arranged the parts in the body, every one of them, just as He wanted them to be* (1 Corinthians 12:18).

The Scriptures teach us that there is both human and divine affirmation. A leader without the respect of the people he leads may be genuinely called of God but is ineffective until recognized by the people. If there is no confirmation by the people, the timing is probably wrong. He needs to wait prayerfully for further instructions from the Lord, trusting God to open and close doors and reveal His will both to him and others.

Pursuing the Call

It is a real privilege to be called by the Lord to serve His people as a small group or house church leader. It's also encouraging to know that the Lord calls average people like you and me. Remember, many of His disciples were common fishermen.

The call to small group and house church ministry is a holy calling and is not to be taken lightly. Paul said, *". . . I urge you to live a life worthy of the calling you have received"* (Eph. 4:1). Leading a small group or house church is a vital work in the Body of Christ, and it offers the wonderful reward of seeing lives changed by the power of the Holy Spirit!

In Philippians 3:14, Paul responded to new areas God was leading him into by saying, *"I press on toward the goal to win the prize for which God has called me heavenward in Christ Jesus."* This is the attitude we need to have as we sense God calling us to lead.

Qualifications for a Leader

The most important thing a small group or house church leader needs to know is that God has called him to that work. The leader has received authority from the Lord and from the local leadership who have acknowledged and appointed him. In addition to being assured of his call, it is crucial that a small group or house church leader has a heart of humility toward those whom he is serving. A test as to whether he has passed this requirement is very simple. Has this leader been willing to serve under someone else's leadership, especially someone he hasn't always agreed with while at the same time pursuing peace, unity, and agreement? If he has, he will probably have the grace that is needed to lead with humility.

You don't have to be a Bible college or seminary graduate to fulfill the requirements of leading a small group of believers. The best kind of leader is simply one who is willing to be a servant to God's people in the small group or house church and share with them the love of Jesus Christ. Leaders serve the believers in the small group and house church in practical ways and also encourage them to hear from God and trust Him to meet their needs. Our availability is often more useful to God than our ability.

Our availability is often more useful to God than our ability.

If someone comes to a DCFI church with the schooling and knowledge to lead, it does not mean he or she is immediately qualified to be a small group leader. We believe it is important to give a person time to *serve* in a small group before he is entrusted with the greater responsibility of *leading* a small group or house church.

In business, the manager who is most effective in giving leadership to a company is the one who actually has experience in the particular field.

That person knows the "ins and outs" of such work, and the problems and challenges that will be faced. The same is true in the church.

This vital truth needs to be balanced with a proper understanding of God's grace and servanthood. If not, it can lead to a performance mentality and selfish ambition. This may be accepted in the business world but is obviously unacceptable in the church.

A true leader has a servant's heart and is willing to take the time needed to be joined and held together with the people in his small group or house church. Ephesians tells us:

> From Him the whole body, joined and held together by every supporting ligament, grows and builds itself up in love, as each part does its work (Ephesians 4:16).

If I were to break a bone, it would take several weeks for the bone to heal and be held together. The church is built by relationships, and it takes time for relationships to be joined together.

Leaders Have a Clear Testimony

If you are called to be a leader, you must have a clear testimony about your salvation, water baptism, and being filled with the Holy Spirit. Areas of healing and deliverance that you have personally experienced should also be part of your testimony. Paul was clearly convinced about his story, *"...I know whom I have believed, and am convinced that He is able to guard what I have entrusted to Him for that day"* (2 Tim. 1:12).

Tell your own story to your small group or house church with a sense of expectancy that God will use it to build faith in His people. Not only is faith built, but often God's Spirit will move and people will be bound together in a special way after candid testimonies are discussed. After one small group leader shared his testimony, a woman, new to the group, and sensing God's compassion and love in the room, broke down and sobbed as she revealed the pain of giving up her child for adoption as a young pregnant teenager. The small group members were able to put their arms around her as God healed those emotions she had buried deep inside for years. It all started with a small group leader simply sharing freely how God had saved, healed, and delivered him of hurts in the past.

Leaders should also be able to explain regularly how God is continuously working in their lives. They should have a testimony that is current because of the vital relationship they have with Jesus Christ.

Leaders Are Full of Faith

Small group and house church leaders must be people who are full of faith and full of the Holy Spirit. Stephen was known as a man with these qualities.

> *This proposal pleased the whole group. They chose Stephen,*
> *a man full of faith and of the Holy Spirit...* (Acts 6:5).

As a small group or house church leader, you will need to exercise your faith by using your spiritual gifts as well. How can a leader help someone else experience spiritual gifts if he does not exercise those gifts himself? For example, if the leader is not hospitable, many times the people in the small group or house church will not learn the importance of hospitality. If the leader doesn't discuss his experience about being filled with the Holy Spirit, the believers in the group will not think it is very important to be filled with the Holy Spirit. If the leaders do not prophesy and exercise spiritual gifts, the small group or house church members probably will not prophesy or exercise spiritual gifts either.

We speak what we know, but we impart who we are. If you find yourself lacking in some of these areas, talk to your local pastor or spiritual parent. They can lead you to someone who has a special anointing in the area you are lacking. An "anointing" is the overflowing life of Jesus that imparts supernatural strength to a person in a particular area.

I've heard it said, "Anointing comes by association." Associate yourself with individuals that God uses. Samuel received his anointing with the association of Eli the priest. The 12 disciples received their anointing from their association with our Lord Jesus Christ. Spend time with a person who has the particular anointing you desire to grow in, and expect the Lord to use you in the same way. That's what faith is all about.

As a young Christian, I had an intense desire to see the Lord move supernaturally. I saw so many people in bondage that needed to be set free, yet I often felt helpless to do anything about it. I knew the Bible said that Jesus Christ is the same yesterday, today, and forever, but I seldom saw the Lord manifest His power in a supernatural way. I then met some friends who were experiencing the Lord's power at work. People were delivered from demons and set free from the oppression of the enemy. I began to spend time with these friends. I watched and prayed as they ministered to others. Before long I was experiencing in my own life the same power that comes through the name of Jesus. Young men and women who came to me for help were being set free.

Leaders Support the Vision of the Local Church

All families do things differently, and we need to be convinced that the vision of our church is one we can embrace as our own so we can enthusiastically carry out our part in its fulfillment. This is why we encourage all our leaders to be well acquainted with DCFI's Biblical Foundation Series, so they clearly understand the mandate the Lord has given to us.

There are probably no two believers on the face of the earth who agree about everything. If there is any aspect of the ministry of a local church or house church network that a small group leader or house church leader cannot consent to or support, he should "share his heart" with his leadership. We need to appeal to those over us in the Lord when we are having difficulty with an area in our lives or in the life of the church.

Many times the Lord will use our appeal to authority to bring change in an area of the church that needs modification.

If a leader is rebellious or divisive, he cannot display the kind of loyalty toward his local church or house church network that the people need to see exhibited.

> *I appeal to you, brothers, in the name of our Lord Jesus Christ, that all of you agree with one another so that there may be no divisions among you and that you may be perfectly united in mind and thought* (1 Corinthians 1:10).

A lack of loyalty to the Word of God and to the local church will cause great harm to the sheep. Some will be confused and others may even scatter to seek other leaders because of their confusion. Sometimes new believers may get involved in cults and deception because of the influence of Christians who appeared to be more mature and sowed seeds of doubt about their local church or its leadership.

If you are serving as a small group or house church leader and find yourself having a wrong spirit toward those in spiritual leadership over you, ask the Lord for grace to correct your attitude, or if you cannot seem to find freedom, then sit down with your leaders and discuss your struggle. When we confess our faults one to another and pray for one another, we can receive healing in these areas (see James 5:16).

The Scripture tells us that whatever we sow, we shall also reap (see Gal. 6:7). We will find people under our spiritual care responding to us in the same way we have responded to those who are over us in the Lord. If we are loyal, others will be loyal to us. If we have a wrong attitude, people under our spiritual care will have the same type of attitude.

Just because our opinion differs with another person in leadership over a certain situation does not mean we are rebellious or that we cannot remain loyal. God wants us to pray about the difference of understanding we have and then talk about it with the appropriate leadership He has placed in our lives.

I've been thankful for the many times believers in the church have shared areas in which they thought we should change as a church. Some of these ideas were implemented and brought great blessing to our family of churches. It is much easier for a person in authority to receive input from one who has prayed and has a teachable spirit. It is spiritually healthy for us to appeal to the authorities God has placed in our lives.

A Leader Is Personable and Easy to Approach

Small group and house church leaders must learn to be "people oriented." A leader's attitude should be, "I will lay down my life to see the believers in our group become men and women of God." Matthew Henry, in his famous commentary on the Bible, says, "Those whose business it is to instruct people in the affairs of their souls should be humble, mild, and easy of access."[1] A good leader cannot think, "I'll lead the meeting and teach the Bible, but I don't want to be bothered all week with everyone's problems." That group is destined to die. Leaders must always be of the attitude, "I'm here to help!" They must be accessible.

Of course, as a leader, you are not called to do everything. Learn to delegate. People learn best by doing. The goal of every small group or house church leader should be to work himself out of a job, as others' talents and gifts are multiplied.

The leader should primarily be a facilitator, rather than the person who is doing everything. Perhaps you could write down the different roles and responsibilities needed for the group to function effectively. Then ask each member to pray about how their gifts might be used in carrying out these various areas of responsibility.

Ask people in your small group or house church questions in order to gain insights into how they feel about your group and about your leadership. Some questions you may ask are, "If you were me, what would you do differently?" "How can I better serve you?" "What areas in your life can I pray with you about?"

Leaders Are Enthusiastic

It is vitally important that you genuinely care for the people in your small group or house church and are enthusiastic about serving them. Your enthusiasm to serve Jesus and others will rub off on those in your group.

> **It is vitally important that you genuinely care for the people in your small group or house church and are enthusiastic about serving them.**

Pastor Cho says that the first qualification of a leader is to be enthusiastic about the things of God. Enthusiasm is contagious. People want to follow someone who leads energetically. They will sense that God's work is important to you when they see you putting your whole heart into it. The Bible says:

> *And whatever you do, do it heartily, as to the Lord and not to men* (Colossians 3:23).

We are commanded by the Lord to do everything with enthusiasm! An enthusiastic leader will produce enthusiastic Christians in his group.

Leaders Have a Gift to Lead People and Recognize Others With That Gift

Where do hurting sheep go? They go to a shepherd. Just as sheep follow shepherds, people are naturally drawn to those in the church who have a genuine gift of leadership. As a leader, God will supply you with

131

the grace you will need to carry out what He has called you to do or insight into the proper resources.

Small group and house church leaders need to be constantly on the lookout for others in their group with a gift of leadership. If you notice that people are attracted to Sarah because she genuinely cares about them and serves them faithfully, encourage those leadership qualities in Sarah. Ask the Lord if He may be instructing you to ask Sarah if she would pray about being an assistant leader of your group in the future. God may eventually call her to lead a small group or house church after she receives on-the-job training.

A Leader Should Not Be a Novice

A new Christian should not be a small group or house church leader, in the same way a 3-year-old child cannot be a baby-sitter. Before a new convert to Christianity can be a leader he needs time and experience before being entrusted with taking care of others. The Bible confirms this in First Timothy 3:6, *"He must not be a recent convert, or he may become conceited and fall under the same judgment as the devil."*

Elisha was trained by Elijah. Timothy was trained by Paul. In each case, the training took a reasonable amount of time. In the business world, workers and executives alike receive training before assuming responsibility. In the church, local leadership is responsible to discern when someone is trained and ready to lead. Each case will be different.

One possibility for new Christians who want to serve in leadership is to have them start as an assistant leader. In this role they are essentially "leaders in training." Within the small group or house church they can get the practical, hands-on training they'll need to help them grow.

When an assistant leader is learning during this apprenticeship period, he or she must be allowed to fail. Small group and house church leaders must remember that they, too, made mistakes as they progressed through the learning process. If they don't forget what they went through as they matured, they will not be tempted to adopt unreasonable expectations for the leaders who come after them. A small group and house church leader's goal should be to support his assistant leaders in success and failure alike and to continue to train them in love.

Married Leaders Are in Unity With Their Spouses About Their Decision to Lead

It's important that leading a small group or house church does not cause disunity in a marriage. The spouse should not only confirm his or her partner's call to serve, but if possible, should be actively engaged in serving the small group or house church as well.

The Scriptures affirm that God uses both men and women as small group and house church leaders. Priscilla and Aquila worked together as a team in the New Testament (see Rom. 16:3). It is quite possible that Priscilla was the one giving leadership to the people God placed within her spiritual care, while her husband supported her.

Many times we have seen the Lord use women in a leadership role in the home group and house church setting, while their husbands play a supporting role. Small group leaders Ken and Kim are a married couple having roles like this. Kim, the more verbal of the two, bubbles with enthusiasm and is gifted in teaching and hospitality. She usually leads the meetings, plans activities, teaches, and generally keeps things rolling. Ken is quiet and prefers to work behind the scenes. A compassionate man, he opens his heart and house to those in the group and is always available to lend a helping hand or to pray with someone. This husband-and-wife team complements each other and flows together in unity.

In a situation where a potential small group or house church leader has a spouse who has not made a decision to follow Christ, it is wise to gain the spouse's agreement before serving in leadership. If a couple is newly married, please note that leading a small group or house church is an added responsibility. Some newlyweds may or may not be ready for this challenge.

Leaders Tithe to the Local Church

*"Bring the whole tithe into the storehouse, that there may be
food in My house. Test Me in this," says the Lord Almighty,
"and see if I will not throw open the floodgates of heaven
and pour out so much blessing that you will not have room
enough for it"* (Malachi 3:10).

The storehouse is the place where God's people bring their tithes and offerings. A tithe is 10 percent of our income. This is a part of God's plan to supply the needs of the spiritual leadership and paid workers of the local church, the house church network and missionaries that are sent throughout the world.[2]

Wherever we invest our money is where our true interests lie. *"For where your treasure is, there your heart will be also"* (Matt. 6:21). Our hearts should be in our local church, including our own small group. We need to support it with our money and our time.

Whether or not we give our tithe to our local church is a clear barometer of our commitment to the church where we are placed. It is easy to say we are committed to the church, but if we are not willing to tithe to the "storehouse," we probably need to reconsider the depth of this commitment.

Some people believe tithing is an Old Testament practice that is not observed in the New Testament; however, Jesus speaks of tithing clearly in Matthew:

Woe to you, teachers of the law and Pharisees, you hypocrites! You give a tenth of your spices—mint, dill and cummin. But you have neglected the more important matters of the law—justice, mercy and faithfulness. You should have practiced the latter, without neglecting the former (Matthew 23:23).

If small group and house church leaders are not tithing to their own local church or house church network, they find it very difficult to teach this biblical principle with conviction to those in their group, since they are not applying it to their own lives. Of course, we do not tithe out of obligation or because of the law, but out of the desire of our hearts to be obedient to the Lord, and in order to see His Church advance.

Leaders Are Accountable

Obey your leaders and submit to their authority. They keep watch over you as men who must give an account. Obey them so that their work will be a joy, not a burden, for that would be of no advantage to you (Hebrews 13:17).

What is accountability? The word *accountability* literally means "to give an account." In our own individual lives, we are accountable to the Lord regarding how we live out our commitment to Christ. Our lives need to "line up" with the Word of God. Personal accountability is not having others tell us what to do. Personal accountability is finding out from God what He wants us to do and then requesting those who are willing to "hold us accountable" to those things.

Many times I have asked others to approach me about "giving an account" to them regarding a goal I believe the Lord set for me. Years ago, I asked one of the men in our small group to hold me accountable with my personal time in prayer and in meditating on God's Word each day. Every morning at 7:00 A.M. I received a phone call as my friend checked up on me. Accountability enabled me to be victorious.

Sometimes we are held accountable for responsibilities that have been delegated to us by others whom the Lord has placed over us. For instance, employees are held accountable by their employers. In the New Testament, Paul the Apostle held those churches whose foundations he had labored to establish accountable to continue to build on Jesus Christ. Paul expected the leaders of these churches to "give an account" to himself and to the Lord for the way they were living their lives. Since the small group leader in a cell-based church is an extension of the leadership of the local church, the small group leader is accountable to the leadership the Lord has placed in His Church. House church leaders are accountable to leaders of the house church network to which the Lord has called them to serve.

One way for us to discern whether or not we are placed properly in the Body of Christ is to ask ourselves this question: Is it a joy to be accountable to the Lord and to our spiritual leaders for our Christian walk and for the way we serve in the Body of Christ? If being accountable to our spiritual leaders is burdensome, we may be improperly placed in the Body of Christ.

True accountability consists in someone loving us enough to check up on us, to see how we are doing in our personal lives and how those in our group are doing spiritually and relationally. I am grateful when those the Lord has placed in my life ask me about my relationship with my wife and children, or hold me accountable for my prayer life—it helps to keep me on track.

In a cell-based church, the leadership team of the local church is ultimately responsible before the Lord for those in the small groups. The small group leader, then, is an extension of the leadership team of the local church. The elders in the local church "give an account" to the Lord for those under their spiritual oversight. Small group leaders serve and assist the elders by ministering to God's people within the small group over which they have charge. In a house church, however, the leaders of the house church are responsible before the Lord for those in the house church in which they serve.

It is important for both small group leaders and house church leaders to converse regularly and to pray with those giving them spiritual oversight. In this way, they are being accountable for their particular area of service and the well-being of those in their group. Accountability is one of the greatest protections God has given us individually and as a church. Each one who is called into leadership in the Body of Christ should be accountable to the Lord and to the servant leaders He has established in His Church. The senior leader of each local church or house church network and the leadership team he represents need to be accountable for their actions, not only to the Lord, but also to others in the Body of Christ. This accountability may be to other leaders in the denomination or "apostolic fellowship" to which the church he represents is connected. Or he may be accountable to other church leaders in his community. Better yet, he may be accountable to both.

The Kind of People God Calls to Leadership

Let's take a look at the kind of people God calls into leadership. This may surprise you! Let's start with Moses:

> *"So now, go. I am sending you to Pharaoh to bring My people the Israelites out of Egypt."*
> *But Moses said to God, "Who am I, that I should go to Pharaoh and bring the Israelites out of Egypt?"*
> *And God said, "I will be with you..."* (Exodus 3:10-12).

Moses was basically saying, "Who am I?" Most leaders feel this way when the Lord calls them to any type of leadership. The first time I was ever asked to pray publicly, I read my prayer off a piece of scratch paper. I was scared! The first small group I led seemed like a monumental task. But I took a step of faith. Joshua did too.

> *Have I not commanded you? Be strong and of good courage; do not be afraid, nor be dismayed, for the Lord your God is with you wherever you go* (Joshua 1:9).

The Lord had to encourage Joshua continually in his new role as a leader. We do not depend on our ability but upon His ability in us! Gideon also struggled with the Lord's call to leadership in His life:

> *"But sir," Gideon replied, "if the Lord is with us, why has all this happened to us? Where are all His wonders that*

*our fathers told us about when they said, 'Did not the Lord
bring us up out of Egypt?' But now the Lord has abandoned
us and put us into the hand of Midian."*

*The Lord turned to him and said, "Go in the strength
you have and save Israel out of Midian's hand. Am I not
sending you?"*

*"But Lord," Gideon asked, "how can I save Israel? My
clan is the weakest in Manasseh, and I am the least in my
family."*

*The Lord answered, "I will be with you, and you will
strike down all the Midianites together"* (Judges 6:13-16).

Jeremiah felt the same way many small group youth leaders feel when
they begin to lead a small group:

*"Ah, Sovereign Lord," I said, "I do not know how to speak;
I am only a child."*

*But the Lord said to me, "Do not say, 'I am only a child.'
You must go to everyone I send you to and say whatever I
command you. Do not be afraid of them, for I am with you
and will rescue you," declares the Lord* (Jeremiah 1:6-8).

Each of these men felt a profound sense of inadequacy when the Lord
called them to leadership. That is the type of person the Lord seeks to
use—those who are completely dependent on Him! According to the
Bible, God delights in manifesting His strength through the weak. In
Second Corinthians 12:9 (NKJV), the Lord tells us, *"...for My strength is
made perfect in weakness."*

If you feel like you may be called to small group leadership, house
church leadership, or to church leadership within any sphere, but you
don't think you have all the natural gifts you need or feel you have made
too many mistakes, be encouraged—you are in good company!

Remember, man looks at the outward appearance, but the Lord looks at the heart. When our heart is in the right place, in complete submission to Him, it is amazing what the Lord can do to prepare and equip us for the responsibilities that lie ahead. Leaders who walk in a healthy sense of inadequacy know they serve a God who is more than adequate.

QUESTIONS TO THINK ABOUT
From Chapter 9

1. Comment on the statement: "Our availability is often more useful to God than our ability."

2. If you are a small group or house church leader, to whom are you accountable?

3. What was the characteristic response of the men God called to leadership in the Bible (Moses, Gideon, and Jeremiah)?

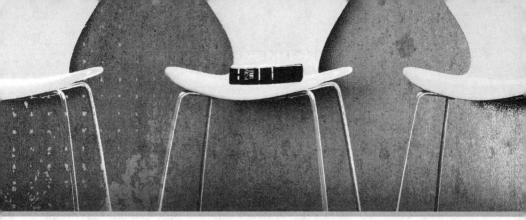

CHAPTER 10

The Responsibilities of Leaders

*I looked for a man among them who would build up
the wall and stand before Me in the gap on behalf of the
land so I would not have to destroy it, but I found none*
(Ezekiel 22:30).

God has called us to "stand in the gap" for Christians and those who have not yet made a decision to follow Christ. We are called to pray for people. Since we are encouraged in Scripture to "pray without ceasing," I believe the Lord would be pleased if we purposed in our hearts to see that each one in our group is covered daily in prayer. We should also pray specifically for family members, friends, and acquaintances of those in our group who have not yet accepted Christ.

Leaders Are Responsible to Pray

The challenge that the Lord has set before us is to trust Him, to reach those who do not know Jesus, and to make disciples. This is the basic job description of a small group and house church leader. In accepting the responsibility to encourage and serve a group of believers, our first priority (next to maintaining a close relationship with Jesus and serving our families) is to pray for those the Lord has placed in our group.

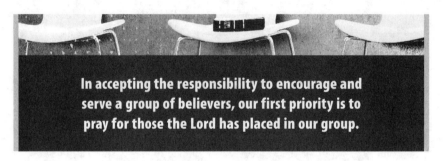

In accepting the responsibility to encourage and serve a group of believers, our first priority is to pray for those the Lord has placed in our group.

Praying is sometimes hard work. Like anything else worthwhile, it must be learned, and learning takes time!

> *My dear children, for whom I am again in the pains of childbirth until Christ is formed in you* (Galatians 4:19).

One of the greatest ways to serve those within the small group and house church is to "labor in prayer" for them. Ask God for direction, and He will show you how to pray diligently for each person.

> *I tell you the truth, whatever you bind on earth will be bound in heaven, and whatever you loose on earth will be loosed in heaven* (Matthew 18:18).

You also need to be involved in spiritual warfare on a regular basis. God has given you the authority to bind the powers of evil and to loose blessing and freedom in the name of Jesus! When praying for the people for whom we are spiritually responsible, it is important that we pray in Jesus' name against any divisive spirits that would try to hinder our group.

> *For our struggle is not against flesh and blood, but against the rulers, against the authorities, against the powers of this dark world and against the spiritual forces of evil in the heavenly realms* (Ephesians 6:12).

Often, individuals don't know they are being influenced by demonic spirits. When people are manipulated by demonic spirits, they may simply seem disinterested or unresponsive to what is going on in the group. In reality, the enemy is hindering them. As a small group or house church leader, you need to "get in your prayer closet" and pray for them in Jesus' name, taking authority over those spirits that are holding them back.

If someone is struggling with a life-controlling problem or openly displaying demonic activity, it is usually best for the small group leaders to meet with this person outside of the meeting. This will give opportunity for further prayer, counsel, ministry, and deliverance. In areas of deliverance from demonic spirits, it is wise to minister two by two whenever possible. If you are not trained, bring someone else who is, but go with the heart of God to learn to minister in this way.

I met a friend in a restaurant one day who was struggling with a habit of smoking cigarettes. He hated it but seemed unable to stop. He was not free to discuss this with the whole group of people in his small group, but he was open with me when we were alone. I prayed for him in the restaurant, and he asked me to take his cigarettes and destroy them. I instructed him to confess the Scripture, *"sin* [cigarettes] *shall have no dominion over me"* (Rom. 6:14). During the next few weeks I checked in on him and encouraged him to continue to trust the Word of God. He was set free. Second Corinthians 10:3-4 says:

For though we live in the world, we do not wage war as the world does. The weapons we fight with are not the weapons of the world. On the contrary, they have divine power to demolish strongholds.

As you serve the people in prayer behind the scenes, your group will experience more unity of spirit and a better atmosphere for spiritual growth.

Praying the Scriptures has been a helpful way for me to pray. When you pray the Word of God, you can know that you are praying the Lord's will. Personalize Scripture with the names of those for whom you are praying. For example: *"I pray that* [Brian's] *love may abound more and more..."* (Phil. 1:9-10). Other excellent "Scripture prayers" to use in praying for spiritual growth among those in your small group or house church can be found in Colossians 1:9-12, Ephesians 1:15-21, and Ephesians 3:14-19.

As believers in Jesus Christ, we can pray with confidence that the Father hears us and will answer our prayers. Philippians 1:6 teaches us to be *"confident of this very thing, that He who has begun a good work in you will complete it until the day of Jesus Christ."* We should pray this truth for those in our small group or house church and for those the Lord is drawing into His Kingdom.

I could give countless illustrations of times when small group or house church members have agreed together in prayer for someone, and God has moved sovereignly to draw that person to Himself. I like to tell the story of two new Christians, Jim and Julie, who began to pray with their small group for the salvation of Jim's father. For years, this man had been angered by any mention of God or religion, but after the group began to pray, Jim noticed that his father began to show an inquisitive attitude toward God. Jim knew the prayers of the believers were not going unnoticed. Then Jim's dad had a terrible accident. In the last hours of his life, while he was still conscious and functioning with a clear mind, a nun at the hospital led Jim's dad to Jesus. Although it was difficult to see a loved one die, Jim and Julie were able to rejoice along with their small group because they knew that the prayers of small group members had played a part in bringing Jim's dad out of the kingdom of darkness and into the kingdom of light.

As a leader, you must set the standard in prayer. Some time ago, I asked the Lord how to have a church that prays. He spoke clearly and said, "*You* pray." A leader must make prayer a priority.

It's important to have someone to pray with whenever possible. Jesus said in Matthew 18:19: *"Again, I tell you that if two of you on earth agree about anything you ask for, it will be done for you by My Father in heaven."*

Pray with your assistant leader(s) on a regular basis. Make sure that you and your assistants are praying for all of your small group members regularly and individually. This will help to alert you and others in leadership to any problems that may accompany the spiritual growth that is occurring in your small group or house church. Pray regularly with your spiritual overseer(s), pastor(s), and those who have been placed over you by the Lord.

Some small groups and house churches find it helpful for each person in the group to have a prayer partner. This may be changed monthly or from time to time. Prayer teams for spiritual warfare are also effective. Small group prayer is important because it helps us to know the heart of others; this fosters spiritual intimacy and strengthens relationships. Remember to pray with expectancy! Through doubt and unbelief, the enemy will try to break our communication line to God.

If your small group or house church seems to be lacking in the area of prayer, have someone come into your group who has an anointing in the area of prayer to teach on the subject and to provide a model of prayer. Prayer is contagious. As you pray with someone who has a "spirit of intercession," your entire group will begin to experience power in prayer. Praying together will also help bring unity to the group.

Leaders Are Called to Make Disciples

Making disciples is the charge that has been given to every believer in the Lord Jesus Christ. Christians call it "The Great Commission." This commission from our Lord Jesus is not an option. We are called to make disciples.

> *Therefore go and make disciples of all nations, baptizing them in the name of the Father and of the Son and of the Holy Spirit, and teaching them to obey everything I have commanded you. And surely I am with you always, to the very end of the age* (Matthew 28:19-20).

Discipleship in its truest sense is not something to be afraid of. It simply means being a friend to someone and helping him or her grow in his or her relationship with God. When Beth, a single mom, joined Cathy's cell group, Cathy at first felt led to pray for Beth and her daughter every day. Cathy and Beth were as different as night and day and seemed to have little in common, but they soon realized that God was bonding them together in a precious way. Cathy became a support system for Beth in her early Christian days. Today, Beth, beautifully matured in Jesus, is often an encouragement to Cathy.

A small group or house church leader who only wants to teach or lead but not be involved in making disciples will not be successful in helping people come to maturity in Christ. Sheep need shepherds, someone who will not only guide them in which way to go but will walk side by side with them, even helping them to carry their load if necessary. Our focus must be on Jesus and helping others become conformed into the image of Christ, not attempting to fulfill our gifts through others.

Leaders Are Called to Encourage, Not to Control

One of the lessons to be learned from history is that small group leaders and house church leaders who are immature or insecure may seek to control God's people rather than encourage them to hear from the Lord for themselves. Our goal must be to present every believer mature in Christ.

The Responsibilities of Leaders

We proclaim Him, admonishing and teaching everyone with all wisdom, so that we may present everyone perfect in Christ (Colossians 1:28).

We need to help the believers in our group learn how to receive direction from the Lord themselves, not encourage them to depend on us by telling them what to do. For example, in considering questions of family finances, family size, child rearing styles, political differences, decisions about standard of living, and so on, a small group or house church leader can give counsel based on his understanding of the Word of God, but such issues, not clearly decided by Scripture, must ultimately be left to the conscience of each believer.

Dr. Cho, in his book *Successful Home Cell Groups,* gives some excellent advice on this subject:

In the past, many home groups have been established outside of the local church and outside of established denominations.... In some cases these independent groups led many Christians into bondage. No one could make a decision unless it was confirmed by the elders of the group. Personal communication with the Holy Spirit was discouraged as those in authority began to exercise greater control over the personal lives of the members, including telling them who they should marry and telling younger members if they were permitted to have contact with their "unbelieving" parents. One of the problems with the independent home groups is that some of them have exercised too much control over their members. That is wrong.

In our church the cell leaders are there to help oversee the spiritual growth of the members, and to encourage them in fellowship and evangelism. But they are never to meddle in the affairs of the members. That is not the responsibility of the church. Each member must be encouraged and taught to depend on the Holy Spirit himself and to develop a life of faith. I never encourage our members to become dependent on the cell leaders...anything that destroys personal independence and the individual's personality and responsibility is from the devil. God never created us to be puppets. He gave us personalities to be developed into loving sons and daughters living in relationship with Him. Our home cell groups are designed to promote that relationship.[1]

The Leader's Leadership Role Is Limited in Four Ways:

1. He cannot deviate in any way from Scripture and still retain his spiritual leadership. (Believers should go to God's Word first to see what God is saying to them before they take the leader's word for it.)

2. He cannot act contrary to the values and guiding principles set by the leadership team of the church or house church network in which he serves and still retain his spiritual leadership. In other words, he cannot act independently outside of his local church authority.

3. He cannot assume the guiding role of the Holy Spirit in the life of another believer. Every believer must ultimately hear from God for himself.

4. He cannot misuse his role of leadership by being abusive, manipulative, or self-serving in any way (for example, by expecting a return for his investment into the lives of people, whether financial, practical, or spiritual).

A Section Leader or Coach—a Small Group Leader Who Oversees Several Small Groups

In a cell-based church, we call a leader who leads his own small group and is also gifted and graced to oversee several other small group leaders, a "section leader, zone leader, or coach." A coach usually is responsible for approximately two to six groups. Many times the groups that a coach oversees have been birthed out of the small group that he leads. In this case, the relationships have already been established between the coach and the small group leaders for whom he is responsible.

A job description for a coach would include praying daily for the leaders he oversees and meeting with the small group leaders for prayer, encouragement, accountability, and spiritual guidance as needed. Coaches also encourage the groups within their section to come together for out-reach—fellowship, picnics, teaching, etc.—as the Holy Spirit leads. They serve the local pastors by sharing their experiences as leaders and clearly communicating their spiritual insights with the small group leaders for whom they are responsible.

Leaders Are Trained and, in Turn, Train Assistants to Help Them

Most DCFI churches have regular small group leaders' training times where leaders are encouraged, learn how to be more effective leaders in their small group, and share testimonies and resources with one another with outreach ideas. Pastors use this *House to House* book as a resource to train new small group leaders. House church leaders also use the *House to House* book to train assistant house church leaders and future leaders.

DCFI churches encourage potential and new small group leaders to go through a one-day training seminar or listen to an audio or DVD series giving a strategy for small groups called "Small Groups 101." Advanced training is also offered in the "Small Groups 201" seminar.[2] For house church leaders and small group leaders, DCFI offers a one-day seminar called "Growing 21st Century Small Groups and House Churches" to train both present and future leaders.[3]

A few years ago, we recognized the need to more effectively train cell-based and house church leaders and church planters. Recognizing this need resulted in starting the "Church Planting and Leadership School." This 135-session leadership training school is producing lasting fruit by giving practical, scriptural leadership tools for both present and future small group leaders, elders, and church planters.

Since many who wanted to receive this training could not move to Pennsylvania to participate in the school, we also produced a video correspondence school in three modules. This training is now being utilized by churches from different denominations and movements throughout the United States, Canada, and in six continents of the world.[4]

Another strategy for training is the one-on-one equipping that takes place when a potential small group or house church leader is discipled by his small group or house church leader. This on-the-job-training is very effective. A potential leader can go along with a leader when he goes to the hospital to pray for the sick. Or the potential leader could join him when he meets with someone who is discouraged and prays a prayer of faith. It has always been a joy for me to lead others to Christ where another believer joins with me as an apprentice and a prayer partner. This way he can witness the miracle of spiritual rebirth right before his eyes. Jesus set the pattern for on-the-job-training. He spent most of His time training a few men, not teaching great crowds. God wants us to train others who will train others—in doing this, we multiply ourselves!

My friend John still talks about the times he joined me witnessing to people in a local park. We walked through the park and took a step of faith in obedience to the Lord as He led us to explain the Good News about Christ with certain individuals. This was a life-changing experience for John.

Small group and house church leaders in training should understand clearly the scriptural principles they learn from training courses, as well as from on-the-job training. They need to be grounded in the Word in order to teach others. Practically speaking, in a cell-based church it is best for a future leader to be regularly involved in small group functions, in weekly celebration meetings, and in personal ministry in the small group setting before beginning to minister as a leader. It is best for future house church leaders to experience serving without a title for a season before becoming a recognized house church leader.

It is also important to remain organized, perhaps using a PDA, an appointment book, or some other type of tool to help remember appointments and to arrive on time. Forgetting an appointment with someone gives the impression that we don't really care about them.

When starting a new small group or house church, the leader should pray for at least one or more assistant leader(s) to serve in the group. Several assistant leaders can be trained at the same time or over a period of time. A scriptural method for training, whether it be for leading people to Christ or for church leadership, is found in Second Timothy 2:2:

> *And the things you have heard me say in the presence of many witnesses entrust to reliable men who will also be qualified to teach others.*

The small group and house church becomes the basic training center for all kinds of ministry. Missionaries do not suddenly and miraculously become trained overnight and leave for foreign fields. They receive training and practice. Job training for leadership must include a hands-on situation. The first qualities to look for in an assistant are those of faithfulness, humility, and the willingness to serve. In fact, in many parts of the world, the only type of church that exists is small group ministry and house church, making it paramount for missionaries to experience small group and or house church ministry as a vital part of their missionary training.

Throughout the past few years we have found three basic types of assistant leaders in small groups and house churches: developmental assistant leaders, perpetual assistant leaders, and catalyst assistant leaders. Here is a brief definition for each type of assistant leader.

1. **Developmental**—those being trained for future leadership. Jesus had 12 assistants, but He seemed to be training Peter as His chief assistant.

2. **Perpetual**—someone who is not a potential primary leader; however, when a small group or house church multiplies, this assistant leader gives a sense of stability and continuity to one of the new groups. This person may always serve in a supportive role and not ever be called to be a primary small group or house church leader.

3. **Catalyst**—someone in church leadership; a person who has a "fivefold ministry gift" or a person who serves as a supported staff person in a church or ministry who is a part of the small group or house church. This person may not be able to take an active role in leadership due to traveling ministry or the responsibility to minister at other small groups or churches. However, this individual proves to be very supportive to the small group or house church leader and is an excellent resource and example of Christ's love within the group.

Process of Confirming New Assistant Leaders

When a small group or house church leader senses that a certain person in the group (let's say Jess) would make an excellent assistant leader, he should initially communicate with his spiritual overseer and other leaders in the group about the possibility of adding a new assistant to help with small group or house church responsibilities. When it is clear after prayer that Jess would be a wise choice, Jess is asked to pray about the possibility of being involved in leadership in the future. If she is married, she and her spouse should be in agreement as well. After Jess is assured that God is calling her and there is a sense of general confirmation from the group, a commissioning service may be planned. Jess is commissioned through the laying on of hands, with prayer from the small group members and someone representing the local church or house church leadership. If any of the local pastors cannot be involved in the commissioning, it is advantageous for those who are absent to make personal contact with Jess to affirm her in her new role.

Assistant Leader's Responsibility to the Leader

Jess's new responsibility as an assistant leader not only involves praying with, but also for, the small group or house church leader to encourage him in his call. She will serve the small group or house church leader in any way she can so that the group is a successful one—that is, one in which people are coming to Christ and being discipled. In the absence of the leader, she will give leadership to the group and look for ways to assist the leader by praying with people, discipling, encouraging, and serving in practical ways. An assistant leader will also bring to the leader's attention areas of concern: potential problems, needs, or "blind spots."

Assistant Cell Leader's Responsibility to Those in the Small Group or House Church

In addition to serving her small group or house church leader, Jess, the assistant, will diligently pray for those in her group. She also helps the leader to contact individuals regularly by phone, texting, email, or in person to comfort, strengthen, and encourage them, giving special oversight and time to the one(s) they are discipling. Some practical ways of serving may include providing rides to meetings as needed, giving group information to members, and giving special care to new believers.

Having a Pastor's Heart

During the early years of DCFI, we called each small group leader the "pastor" of his small group. We have come to believe it was a mistake for us to do that. A small group leader must always be willing to serve those in his group through prayer, encouragement, and relationship; however, he may or may not have the gifting of a pastor. Some leaders are gifted administrators, others are evangelists, others are teachers, and so on.

When we called small group leaders "pastors," some of them got overwhelmed and quit. Others, because of their traditional understanding of the word "pastor," felt like they should have a ministerial license to be a small group leader.

We believe we should call the leaders what they really are. If they are small group leaders, then we should call them that. If they lead a house church, call them house church leaders. In actuality, a small group leader seems to be serving in a deacon-type role. Deacons are ministers (servants to the Body of Christ). If we see them as small group shepherds, then we should call them that. We just need to be sure that the terminology that is used is clearly articulating the vision that the Lord has given to us.

Again, the small group leader is not necessarily expected to be the pastor. He may have some pastoral gifts but should only respond to situations according to his faith. Some small group leaders have a pastoral gift within them and perhaps will be used as pastors with greater spiritual responsibilities in the future. Usually in house churches, the house church leader takes more of a pastoral role, but the house church network leadership is available to assist them in their role of leadership at any time.

On the other hand, every small group or house church leader needs to have a pastor's heart. A person with a pastor's heart has a desire to serve a group of people through prayer, regular encouragement, and practical service, although it does not mean he has the final pastoral responsibility.

A teenager might "mother" her younger brother or sister, but that does not make her the natural mother. Later on, she will be a mother and have her own children. This same principle applies to those who are "pastoring" as small group leaders in a cell-based church. Small group leaders are serving alongside the local pastors and others in leadership in their local area so that every believer can and will be involved in ministering to others.

Set the Example

In the small group or house church setting, the enemy will lie to us at times and tell us that we cannot really help others because we have not "been there." Was Jesus ever on drugs or alcohol? Was He ever divorced? No, of course not, and yet He has provided for us a wonderful example. Regardless of our life experiences, we can pray and trust the living God and see the Lord do miracles among us.

You can set the example by sharing your own personal needs and problems with those in your group. The Bible tells us in Second Corinthians 12:9 that we should boast in our weaknesses so that the power of Christ may rest upon us. When we are open about areas of struggle that we've had and explain how the Lord has given us grace to be victorious, our transparency deters others from placing us on a pedestal. When people put us on a pedestal, we open ourselves to the enemy in the area of pride. People we are serving feel as though they can never attain our level of spirituality, which is totally untrue.

We can minister most effectively by showing the people in our small group or house church the Word of God rather than by giving them our own opinions. If you don't have the answer, don't fake it. Tell them honestly that you don't know, but you will find the answer. That's why God provided spiritual overseers and pastors and other ministry gifts in the Body of Christ.

Remember, the Word of God gives us spiritual authority. Also, your testimony is a powerful tool that the Lord can use to encourage His people in your group. Your testimony is simply relating what God has done in your life in the past, what He is doing in your life now, and what you believe God is going to do in the future.

Leaders should not give strong advice or correction to a person they do not know very well (unless they are clearly led by the Holy Spirit). Much patience is needed before attempting to correct someone's faults. Simply continue to love and care for them, and many times they initiate the desire for advice and help. They will see in you an example of how they themselves want to become.

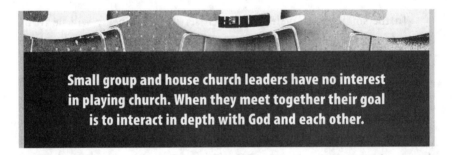

Small group and house church leaders have no interest in playing church. When they meet together their goal is to interact in depth with God and each other.

True leaders will take time—all the time that is necessary—to build good, trusting relationships with people. We must build relationships not only within the setting of the small group or house church meeting, but outside the meeting as well. Through informal occasions spent in social interaction outside of the meeting context, the time will eventually come when you will feel free to speak into the lives of the people in your group because of the trust that has been established. If you don't have a relationship with the people in your group, it will be very difficult for them to receive advice or correction from you.

Small group and house church leaders have no interest in playing church. When they meet together their goal is to interact in depth with God and each other. But even within small group dynamics, there is a need for strategy and guidelines when believers meet collectively. In the next chapter we will look at general guidelines as we allow Christ to express Himself at our meetings.

QUESTIONS TO THINK ABOUT
From Chapter 10

1. Describe the basic job description of a small group or house church leader.

2. In what ways might a leader struggle with control in the small group or house church?

3. List several ways in which a leader is limited in his leadership role.

4. List some ways a leader can give on-the-job training to others.

CHAPTER 11

The Meetings

In a church with small groups (a cell-based church), there are two distinct meetings—the larger Sunday morning celebration service and the small groups that meet during the week in homes. The dynamics of the small group meetings are completely different from the Sunday morning celebration meetings. In the small groups, everyone has the opportunity to share life experiences and openly address others in the group, but the larger celebration is a time for corporate worship and teaching.

In a house church, the dynamic is often much different. House churches work so that each small church functions as a little church, a place where God's people experience community, worship, teaching, and pastoral care. Although healthy house churches normally network with other house churches within a network, the house church is the main focus for the local church and not the network itself.

In light of this, wise house church and small group leaders will ask the Lord for wisdom, knowing that each house church and small group needs to be tailor-made to fit the needs of the people involved. Some need more teaching, some more community, and others need to be challenged to move out in evangelism.

Since both the small group and the house church involve a small number of people, there are not as many spiritual gifts available as there are in a larger meeting. For example, there may not be anyone in the small group or house church gifted as a worship leader, yet at a weekend celebration meeting or network gathering there may be many worship leaders. So then, the purpose of the small group meeting in a cell-based church is not to try to be a miniature celebration meeting, but instead to be a safe environment for the Lord's people to share their lives together, pray, discuss the Word of God, and receive a vision from the Lord to reach those who do not yet follow Christ.

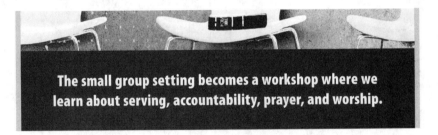

The small group setting becomes a workshop where we learn about serving, accountability, prayer, and worship.

Within a small group setting, learning about "practical Christian living" is anticipated. In small groups we grow in spiritual maturity because we learn to accept and love our brothers and sisters unconditionally. It's a place where we pray for each other's brokenness as we witness the healing work of Jesus. Compassion surrounds us, and encouragement lightens our loads. When we hear what God is teaching others in their personal lives, it teaches us these same principles. The small group setting becomes a workshop where we learn about serving, accountability, prayer, and worship. It is where we can be brought as believers to a place of strength and maturity. We learn about practical Christian living as we watch over one another, knowing that as we serve, we are all growing stronger in Christ.

Choosing a Place for the Meeting for Both Cell Groups and House Churches

Every believer should be involved in the particular small group or house church that would release him to be fulfilled in his walk with God while at the same time serving others. It may or may not be with people in his local community. The church is built by relationships. Even though most people will find themselves serving alongside believers in their own geographical area, they may initially drive many miles to serve with other believers with whom the Lord has placed them for a particular season of time. If a small group or house church receives them, people should have the freedom to go to the group where they believe God has called them, where they feel a unity and oneness or homogeneity with their fellow believers.

Sometime during our early years as a church, we decided to require small group attendees to get involved in a group that was within the closest proximity to where they lived. The principle was right. It is often more effective to relate to the people within our own geographical area rather than drive miles out of the way to attend a small group meeting; however, we soon learned that this advice cannot be dictated. The Holy Spirit is the one who builds people together in relationships. It soon became apparent that some people felt pressured to attend a small group nearby when in reality they had built relationships and felt bonded to others from a more distant small group. Also, this principle didn't work for homogenous small groups, which drew people with the same basic interests and experiences but often from diverse geographical areas.

After we realized that we had made a mistake, we repented and released the people to listen to the Holy Spirit and do what He told them to do. As spiritual leaders, we must be sensitive to those we serve. We constantly have the choice between leading by the letter of the law or by the Holy Spirit. Today it is interesting to notice that most people in our family of churches are involved in a small group or house church in their geographical area. They are in relationship with these people because they want to be, not because church leadership requires it.

When deciding where your small group or house church will meet, the following are some things to consider. Is the location central for the majority of the people in your group? Does it have a large enough room for the group to gather in with space for newcomers? If needed, is there a separate room for children's ministry? Does the place offer a comfortable and relaxing atmosphere to adults and children as well? If the group meets in a home, are the hosts financially able to meet the needs that hosting a group involves? This question is of special significance in cultures where serving coffee, tea, and cookies or biscuits is expected.

Sometimes the small groups and house churches meet in the same home until the group multiplies or the location is no longer suitable. Other groups find it much more advantageous to rotate to various homes of the members. Those who are willing to host the meeting exercise the gift of hospitality and are secure in this capacity to have the church meet in their home.

Meeting Time and Format for Small Groups and House Churches

In the past at DCFI, most small groups met twice a month, and then they were encouraged to meet together to pray during the "off week." Today, many DCFI churches do it differently. Some small groups have found it most effective to meet together each week. Sometimes groups will alternate a regular meeting with an outreach or game night. Other times the women will meet separately from the men on the off weeks. The men or women may get together for breakfast or go bowling. Believers in house churches usually meet together weekly.

Since the small group meeting and relationships are a priority in cell-based churches, believers should be spending at least as much time in some type of a small group context as in other types of church meetings. We are not minimizing the effectiveness of meetings of congregations or larger corporate celebrations. They are also important, but the New Testament church did both. They met in public meetings and from house to house (see Acts 20:20).

It is important that you follow the leading of the Holy Spirit when you conduct your small group and house church meetings. A helpful hint is to be prepared! Have a schedule and stick to it, unless you know that the Spirit is leading otherwise. There is no excuse to say you are "following the Holy Spirit" if in actuality you are unprepared. Many times we say we are Spirit-led when in reality we have been lazy and undisciplined. This is a disgrace to our Lord and to His people. To waste people's time shows poor leadership.

Prayer should be planned as a vital part of your time together. Ask someone beforehand to open with prayer. Have a time for intercession and praise. Give everyone an opportunity to pray. Be helpful and encouraging when people are learning to pray out loud.

One of the men in a small group that I led some years ago was afraid to pray publicly. He knew that he had to deal with this fear. He asked me to request that he pray in front of the other men in the group when we met together every other week before work. As I asked him to pray and encouraged him, he went on to lead various small groups in the years that followed. He just needed some encouragement and accountability in the small group setting.

Teach people to pray. Encourage short conversational prayers. Explain the importance of praying in agreement according to Matthew 18:19-20:

> *Again, I tell you that if two of you on earth agree about anything you ask for, it will be done for you by My Father in heaven. For where two or three come together in My name, there am I with them.*

I am really hesitant to give guidelines for what should happen at a small group or house church meeting because I believe it is so easy to trust the format rather than being truly open to what the Holy Spirit wants you to do. But so many pastors and small group leaders have asked me to discuss these guidelines that I believe I need to address this subject.

Many times small group meetings include a time of worship, testimonies, a short teaching (approximately 15 to 20 minutes), a time for response to the teaching, announcements, prayer, and sharing of life together. The format can be changed and altered in a thousand ways. You do not have to do all of these things, or in reality you do not need to do any of these things. Every time you come together should be different. Do not get stuck in a rut.

Every effort should be made to start and end your meetings on the agreed times. Be respectful of other people's time, especially parents of babies and school children who must study. Unless you are clearly led otherwise, I encourage you to keep the actual teaching and discussion part of the meeting to about one hour.

House Church Meetings

Although there are many similarities between small group meetings and house church meetings, house churches often take a bit of a different approach to their meetings. Some house churches have four basic components to the meeting, including eating, meeting, small groups, and "the meeting after the meeting." Most house church meetings start with a potluck meal as a vital part of the church meeting, and continue on to include a time of worship, teaching, and discussion. Many house church meetings last a total of two to three hours.

One of the problems in some house churches is a lack of biblical teaching. In light of this, many house churches are a part of a house church network and often meet together corporately one time each month for a larger expression of worship and biblical teaching. The time allotted for teaching may be a bit longer in a house church then in a cell group. Teaching can take many forms; from a house church member giving a teaching, to reading and discussing Scripture, to watching a Bible teacher on a DVD, to having a guest in the house church teach from the Scriptures.

If the house church is larger than five to six people, we encourage them to break down into even smaller groups for the last part of the house church meeting to pray for each other and be open with one another often in gender-specific groups. This also provides an excellent training opportunity for future house church leaders to begin to experience spiritual leadership.

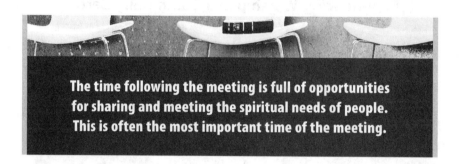

The time following the meeting is full of opportunities for sharing and meeting the spiritual needs of people. This is often the most important time of the meeting.

Finally, "the meeting after the meeting" happens! The time following the meeting is full of opportunities for sharing and meeting the spiritual needs of people. This is often the most important time of the meeting. Those who must leave may go, and those who want to seek help from the leader or others in the group are free to do so. Many times after meetings, clusters of people gather together for informal fellowship to talk heart to heart and pray together. These times are invaluable as our fellow believers surround us with compassion and give us the courage to keep going so we will be able to stand tall, embodying the very fullness of Christ (see Eph. 4:11-16). Here's a good description of this time from a book I co-authored with Floyd McClung, entitled *Starting a House Church:*

> In most conventional churches, people are ready to go home right after the service. Not so in house church. These people love being together. Actual meeting times may last one hour or three or more hours—whatever it takes to allow for adequate participation from everyone.[1]

Whether in a small group or house church setting, we must remember our mission—to pray, reach those who do not trust Jesus and make disciples. Unless we keep our eyes firmly fixed on our mission, we may forget why we are together. The enemy may deceive us and put us to sleep spiritually while the world goes to hell around us.

Experiencing Worship in a Community Setting

Worship is a vital part of any small group, but sometimes we struggle with how to approach it in a smaller group setting because we often try to re-create a traditional Sunday-style worship service. Although the New Testament suggests that Christian worship incorporates the singing of hymns and psalms (see Eph. 5:19), prayer (see 1 Cor. 11:4-5), vocal thanksgiving (see Eph. 5:20; Heb. 13:15), and instruction (see 1 Cor. 14:26; Col. 3:16), in a small group, worship should be far more.

We must understand that what makes us the people of God is the fact that we are a worshiping community. We were created to worship a living God. This means that we are people of worship—a community of people who center ourselves on the Lord. God desires that worship holds a central place in our lives because He wants our hearts. So, in a small group setting, worship is not just singing songs to the Lord in our living rooms. Worship compels us to work through our problems and difficulties of relationships so that when we come before God in praise, we can do so without relational issues getting in the way.

Our act of worship includes the ways in which we live, the ways in which we serve God in our small group or in the community and workplace during the week. We should live as an act of worship that seeks to bring glory to our God and give back to Him the worship He deserves. In the context of worship, everyone can experience God and hear Him speak.

Worship Leaders

If possible, each small group and house church should try to have at least one person designated to lead the group in worship. If a person is selected for this ministry, he does not need to play an instrument—although many do—but should be able to lead in worshipful singing to the Lord.

Worship leaders can also make use of music CDs that enhance the times of singing to the Lord. Cell members and house church participants can be encouraged to come to the meetings with a song or a hymn to share with the group. When everyone feels a sense of responsibility for what happens at the meeting, you can expect the Lord to move through His body in a powerful way.

The worship leader should stick to the allotted time given by the small group or house church leader for the worship period. He also should have song sheets available for new members who would be uncomfortable worshiping without knowing the words.

Ministering to the Children

Many times small groups or house churches that have families with children provide ministry time for the older children or nursery for the younger ones. You could either have a regular leader for the children or have different people in the group take turns. Sometimes people from one small group or house church will serve the children in another group if the two groups meet at different times. Whatever you do, do not place the children in front of the television set as a baby-sitter; however, the use of Christian videos with a responsible teacher is appropriate as a part of the ministry to children.

We think it is best for two people to minister together to the children. In a day when child abuse has reached the proportions that it has (statistics now tell us that one out of every three girls and one in seven boys will be sexually assaulted before they reach the age of 18), two ministering together for the purpose of accountability is advisable.

Some small groups and house churches gear the entire meeting to minister to the families as a whole because they find this format the most advantageous for their group. The children are part of the worship, prayer, sharing, and ministry. We must listen to the Holy Spirit for His direction on these matters. What is right for one group may not be right for another.

When our daughter Charita was 12, she felt a special call to serve the younger children in our small group. She used her organizational and teaching gifts to gather materials together suitable for Bible stories. She planned craft activities and collected prizes to give to the children when they learned their Bible verses, as well as planned skits, puppet shows, and games. The kids loved it and looked forward to coming to the group because they felt included and cared for.

Some small groups and house churches have a special youth night or children's night. On these nights the youth in the group plan the entire meeting. Other times the children may give a special program. Be creative and look to the children to be creative and imaginary. Intergenerational small groups can be the most fun as they incorporate the gifts and maturity levels of each generation.

Release the children to minister to the small group. Children have faith unlike adults many times. Children can lay hands upon the sick and pray for the sick. Children can prophesy and speak into the life of the group. Children can work on a skit to present to the group at the close of the meeting. Jesus embraced children, and so should our small groups and house churches.

Handling the Group's Finances

In cell-based churches, many times small groups take occasional offerings and keep the money available for emergencies in the group. (This is not our tithe but an offering for service to others.) The money is then used by the group to purchase flowers for someone in a hospital or recovering from an illness or to give groceries to a needy family.

It is a good rule of thumb for the small group leader or assistant leader to be the treasurer for this fund. The fund is of great help when money is needed quickly. This way the need to collect money from everyone for each emergency is eliminated. Usually the emergency financial need can be met by the group, but if more help is needed, a network of small groups may get involved.

In house churches, the tithes and offerings are received at the house church. Most house churches serve within the guidelines of their particular house church network so they can properly administrate the funds with integrity and accountability. In cases where a great deal of money is needed and it is beyond that which the local small group or house church can handle financially, the leader is encouraged to contact the local pastor, house church network leaders, or someone who is designated within the local congregation or house church network to handle this responsibility. In some of the DCFI cell-based churches a special "deacon's fund" that is financed by a percentage of the tithes of the church is available to the small group leaders during times of financial need within their group, when the need is greater than the group and its members can handle alone.

Small Group Social Activities

Small group and house church leaders should periodically initiate activities for their groups to further build relationships. Outings, civic tasks, serving others, eating together, and local evangelistic outreaches are just a few examples of the kinds of activities in which a group can participate.

People who are gifted in the area of organization may be assigned to help plan activities. It helps to delegate responsibility to others, because it will give people a sense of kinship for what God is doing. Remember, small groups and house churches are called to be teams, working together to build the Kingdom of God in a given area. And please do not forget, our primary focus needs to be prayer and reaching those who do not yet follow Jesus.

It is not necessary for each activity to include everyone in the group. Believers can get together for a baseball game or for a craft session. There are a great many activities in which to participate in order to reach those who do not yet believe in Christ.

Small groups and house churches can also meet for breakfast or for a meal during a day off or over a lunch break. Another option is to combine activities for an entire section of small groups or a house church network. Before finalizing any plans for a combined event, though, it is best for leaders to check with their local pastor or house church network overseer to make sure this event does not conflict with another church function of which they are unaware.

Birthdays and Anniversaries

Birthdays and anniversaries are an important part of our lives. Some of the believers whom the Lord has placed in your small group or house church may not have a family who cares about them, or their families may live in another state or area. Remembering birthdays, anniversaries, and other special events with cards, an occasional party, etc., can be a tremendous source of encouragement.

Perhaps someone in the small group or house church could compile a list of birthdays and anniversaries that could be photocopied and passed out to the entire group. As the group grows and multiplies, this list will become outdated, but the information can still be used as relationships continue even after multiplication.

Snacks and Food

Most house churches include food as an important part of their house church meetings. Having food can be a real blessing, but care must be taken that it does not become competitive or a burden to anyone. Some small groups only serve snacks on special occasions, such as birthday parties or other celebrations. In some cases, having snacks at the conclusion of each meeting could be distracting to what the Holy Spirit is doing. If you meet in various homes week to week, the person or family that is opening their home may feel pressure to do something that someone else has done but may not have the time or the finances. This could cause unnecessary tension. Be sensitive to the leading of the Holy Spirit and clearly communicate to everyone in your small group or house church what you think the Lord is saying about this.

Water Baptism

Peter replied, "Repent and be baptized, every one of you, in the name of Jesus Christ for the forgiveness of your sins. And you will receive the gift of the Holy Spirit" (Acts 2:38).

God's will is for new believers to be added to the church daily! When a new believer comes into the group, the small group or house church leader should inquire if he was baptized in water. If he has not been, the leader or another believer in the group can serve that person by baptizing him. The local pastor or house church network overseer may also be available to give training in this area. They can help the small group or house church leader with the details of locating a proper place for the baptism. We have used swimming pools, bathtubs, rivers—anywhere there was water available for a baptism. Take this opportunity to teach new believers the purpose of water baptism from the Scriptures.

Water baptism signifies our "death" in Christ and our "resurrection" with Him into new life as we come out of the water. Have a time of prayer for the person. Many times words of prophecy will be given at this time.

Often the entire small group or house church and the person's family will be in attendance, which provides an opportunity for witnessing and celebrating. Sometimes the new convert will give his or her testimony during the baptism. Romans 6:1-10 provides a great text from which to explain the Gospel at the water baptism site.

Communion; Love Feasts

Each small group and house church has the liberty to celebrate the Lord's Supper as often as it wishes in the small group setting. It is a vital part of the Christian life to remember and meditate on the death and resurrection of our Lord Jesus Christ. Paul stressed it was the most important issue he could preach, *"...Jesus Christ, and Him crucified"* (1 Cor. 2:2).

It is important that the communion time is worshipful, with a sense of celebration. The leader can read or discuss passages such as First Corinthians 11:23-26, or passages on the Last Supper from the Gospels, about the death and resurrection of Jesus. Sometimes it can be very meaningful to have someone in the group sing a special song or background music could be played to encourage the people as they share communion together.

Some of the house churches and small groups in DCFI churches have had a meaningful and spiritual time of washing each other's feet as a symbol of servanthood, or some have had a love feast (a meal together) as found in John 13. Care must be given to properly explain and adequately prepare for such special times, but the outcome can be a tremendous blessing for each member of the group.

Baby Dedication

I prayed for this child, and the Lord has granted me what I asked of him. So now I give him to the Lord. For his whole life he will be given over to the Lord. And he worshiped the Lord there (1 Samuel 1:27-28).

When a newborn is dedicated to the Lord, it is a special time for the entire group as well as for relatives of the child who may not be a part of the small group, the house church, or the local congregation. It can be a time of joy and a powerful testimony. The group should affirm their willingness to help the parents in training the child for the glory of God.

Sometimes the small group or house church leader will read the story of the infant Jesus' dedication found in Luke 2 and allow the parents to express their commitment to bring up the child in the loving discipline and instruction of the Lord.

In a cell-based church, the small group leader should communicate with the local pastor regarding the new baby's dedication in the small group setting. At times, baby dedications are handled at the congregational level and other times at the small group level. Sometimes both are settings are used.

How Many People Should Be in a Group?

Jesus' small group consisted of 12 disciples. Moses encouraged small groups of ten. Ten to twelve adults in a group seems to be an ideal number of people to serve together. New groups only need a few people to start. If two or three gather in His name, He is in their midst! When the group grows to 20 or more adults, it can become a bit too large to be effective. The key to starting new groups is leadership. If leadership is not adequately prepared to start a new small group or house church, wait until leaders are properly equipped. People who are involved in small groups without clear leadership often become disillusioned.

One of our small groups a few years back had more than 80 people in it. That group was larger than the average church in America! But we had to wait until leadership was released for the group to multiply.

When a group becomes large, another unforeseen problem may come into existence. Where do you park all the cars when you meet together at someone's home residence? Often the overflow spills onto the side of the street or road and can be a potential problem for neighbors. In this case, we suggest that members try to carpool whenever possible. Respect for the community must always be observed. Cars should never be parked where they interfere with traffic flow or neighbors' properties.

Commissionings

Whenever someone in the small group or house church is going out on a mission trip, or into a ministry, or moving to another small group or area, the entire group is given opportunity in commissioning them out. This commissioning should not take place on the spur of the moment. It should be announced well in advance so that no one is taken by surprise. During the time of commissioning, have the members lay their hands on the person or persons, and as many as are led by the Lord should pray. At this time, prophecy and words of wisdom and knowledge may also be given.

Commissionings are also encouraged when multiplying a new small group and house church or when confirming new leaders or assistant leaders from within the group. Communication with the local pastor or house church network overseer prior to this is important. If the pastor or overseer can be involved in the commissioning, it gives the Lord's people a sense of being linked to a movement of God, not just to a small group of people.

We believe that many Christians in the future will see the church as believers meeting in clusters of small groups in a given locality. These clusters of small groups and house churches will network together with other congregations to affect their communities for Jesus Christ. By concentrating on relationships rather than structure, small groups and house churches give everyone an opportunity to be involved, and people feel like they are part of a family.

In the next chapter, we will take a look at a variety of leadership skills an individual needs to lead a small group or house church so that members can experience healthy community in the group and also a clear vision to multiply.

QUESTIONS TO THINK ABOUT
From Chapter 11

1. When a specific need of a small group or house church member is communicated to the leader(s), what steps can be taken to help meet this need?

2. What can a small group do to minister to the children? How can the children minister to the group?

3. When some members of a small group or house church sense that they are to join another group, what can the present leaders do to honor this person?

CHAPTER 12

Skills for Leading

Be Flexible and Creative

To keep the meetings vibrant, don't settle into a dull routine. Plan well ahead for new activities. Talk with other small groups and house churches to find out what they are doing. Ask the people in your group periodically for suggestions. Resource books such as *Creative Ideas for Cell Groups* and *Starting a House Church* can be helpful resources for you.[1]

On occasion, when someone in the group is in need, go to his or her home to help him or her instead of having the regular meeting. One night our small group met, and we realized that the one couple was missing because they had fallen behind in their yard work. Rather than scolding them for missing the meeting, we laid aside our plans for the meeting and went to their home and helped them. It was a tremendous time ministering to them in a practical way.

Other times we have joined another small group (or the whole section or house church network) for an evening together. These kinds of alternatives help keep the group flexible.

Call People by Their Names

In America, it is important that you know the people in your group on a first-name basis. Although other nations and cultures may require the use of proper names or family names, Americans usually address people by their first name as a common courtesy. In a small group setting, this kind of friendly familiarity draws people out and encourages them to participate. As you make use of illustrations and parables as you teach, employ the names of the people in the group as often as possible. It makes people feel important, and they should, because God thinks they are!

Jesus, the Good Shepherd, knows each of His sheep and calls them by name. As the leader spends time in prayer for each person in his group on a daily basis, he will find it will not take long until he knows each name by heart.

In case you have real difficulty remembering names, here is a helpful tip: When meeting someone and hearing his name for the first time, think of someone else you know who has the same name. It could be the name of a friend or family member or a character in the Bible. Then remember that name every time you think of the new person until you have it memorized.

Don't Put People on the Spot

Try to get everyone to participate in the meeting; however, it is important that you do not embarrass people by having them read Scripture, or pray, or explain a verse if they are uncomfortable with this. Some people in the small group or house church you may know well enough to be certain that they would not object. If you are not sure, you should ask them prior to the meeting. Give them the freedom to decline if they need to.

I have a friend who was put on the spot in a Sunday school class as the class members were reading the Scriptures one person at a time. My friend had difficulty reading and was so uncomfortable and embarrassed that it took 20 years to get enough courage to go back to a Sunday school class. A sensitive leader could have saved my friend a lot of pain.

Ask Johnny if he is willing and ready to give a public testimony before telling the group he has something to share. Encourage timid Christians to be open, but speak with them privately about it first.

These introverted or shy people are best reached by gaining their confidence after the meeting. If there is someone who sits in the corner and hesitates to join in, make a point of spending time with him in casual conversation a few times and gradually enlist him to take part in the meeting and activities. Remember how you felt when you were a new Christian.

Teaching Tips

In the small group setting in a cell-based church, people do not gather to receive "deep teaching." Such in-depth teaching can be received at the larger celebration meetings (where there is a focus on teaching God's Word), at training events, through reading books and listening to teaching CDs. A teaching presented during the meeting should be short, with comments and response for practical application. We recommend that these messages last about 10 to 15 minutes.

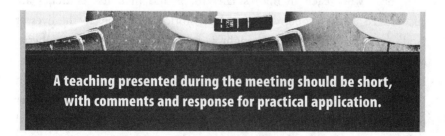

A teaching presented during the meeting should be short, with comments and response for practical application.

Since it could become a burden for many small group leaders to study and prepare a new teaching for each meeting, some churches provide CDs containing a Bible teaching, along with a set of notes for the small group leader, well in advance of the meetings. The leader then is responsible to get the teaching into his spirit first, as preparation, before teaching it. This resource allows the small group leader, who is probably working a full-time job, to put more time into prayer and practical discipleship.

A prepared teaching is not a requirement to teach, but an option as each leader prays about what the Lord wants the group to do together each week. The leaders are encouraged, however, to study the teaching that is prepared as personal training and development for them as leaders even if they don't use it to teach. Some churches provide notes from the Sunday sermon to use in small group teaching and discussion times. In a house church, teaching is often more important since the believers do not receive biblical teaching each Sunday at a weekend service.

Every small group and house church is at a different place spiritually. If the people in the group are largely new believers, the teachings should be much different compared to a group that has all mature believers who need to be motivated and stirred to reach those who do not yet believe Christ.

When I served as senior pastor, members of our small groups received further training by signing up to take extended training courses we offered throughout the year, including biblical teaching on marriage,[2] personal finances, teachings applicable to youth, training children, prayer, operating in the gifts of the Spirit, evangelism, church planting, etc. This provided ample opportunity to receive specific biblical training.

Those who teach in both small groups and in house churches are encouraged to use modern-day parables, stories that apply to the lives of God's people. Jesus constantly taught with stories. The people remembered the story, and then they remembered the spiritual truth. A key to teaching is to be a good storyteller. Some years ago I developed an interest in Dwight L. Moody, the famous evangelist of the 19th century. I remember my amazement when I picked up a book of his sermons. They were filled with stories. John Wesley used to rehearse his sermons in the presence of his 9-year-old servant girl. If she could understand it, then he would give the message publicly.

Again, I want to emphasize that each small group and house church is encouraged to do whatever is most effective for their group to be reaching those who do not yet believe in Christ and making disciples. If someone needs healing in the group or has a friend who is sick, perhaps there should be a short teaching on healing with a time of prayer for the sick.

Some small groups and house churches may listen to a CD or watch a DVD of a teaching. Then they take their Bibles and discuss the truths that were taught and help one another apply them to their personal lives. Other small groups and house churches have used DCFI's Biblical Foundation Series books[3] as teaching formats or used other printed materials.

Another refreshing thing that can happen is to invite a person with the spiritual gift of apostle, prophet, evangelist, pastor, or teacher into your small group or house church to minister to God's people. These "circuit riders" can impart more under the anointing of the Holy Spirit in one evening than you could imagine. The question to ask is: What will be the most effective thing for our group to do for every person to know Jesus in an intimate way and fulfill the Great Commission?

Maintain Order

Keep the meeting moving and alive. Whoever has been given responsibility for a particular part of the meeting must be enthusiastic about his part, or the meeting will falter and be of no benefit. People will be bored.

If there are those who constantly interrupt, they should be gently confronted with the truth that they need to "consider others as more important than themselves." First Corinthians 14:26 tells us:

> *What then shall we say, brothers? When you come together,*
> *everyone has a hymn, or a word of instruction, a revelation,*
> *a tongue or an interpretation. All of these must be done for*
> *the strengthening of the church.*

Nothing should be permitted to take place that does not line up with the Scriptures or quenches the Holy Spirit. For example, one evening I was leading a meeting when one of the men began to "pray" in a tongue that sent chills up my spine. There was something drastically wrong. I turned the meeting over to someone else and along with another Christian brother took this man into another room to minister to him. It became apparent that he needed deliverance and the voice he was "praying" in was the voice of a demon.

If you feel that your meetings are getting out of hand because one person monopolizes the time, you may need to encourage that person who is overly verbal to allow others time to talk. Ask him to stick to a time limit.

If someone takes the meeting "down a side street" by getting off the subject, you can tactfully tell him that you will be happy to talk to him privately about it after the meeting. This way you can honor him as a person, and you can keep the meeting from becoming boring for the rest of the people.

Utilize Gifts of the Spirit

Each person in the small group and house church should be learning how to be sensitive to the Holy Spirit's promptings. For example, the leader should encourage each person to contribute to the supernatural life of the group. A close-knit group will provide an ideal setting to step out and begin exercising the gifts of the Spirit. As God directs, the leader needs to be sensitive and remember that it is a bit scary to give a prophecy or a word of knowledge for the first time.

The first time that I prophesied I was in a group of three people. I was so scared, my palms were sweaty, but at the encouragement of my two brothers in Christ I took a step of faith and prophesied for the first time.

Often the Holy Spirit will activate gifts in people during a time of worship or prayer, but opportunity must be given for the Holy Spirit to do His work. Invite Him to come among you and give Him liberty to operate in the group.

The Holy Spirit may give one person a prophecy. He may give another a word of wisdom or a word of knowledge (see 1 Cor.12:8). He may call you to take some time for gifts of healing or the working of miracles to flow.

The gifts of the Holy Spirit have been given to us to edify the church, to minister to those who have not yet accepted Christ, and to confound the unbelieving (see 1 Cor. 14). The small group or house church is the place for training and releasing the gifts of the Holy Spirit so that these gifts become a part of our everyday lives as we reach out in faith to pray for miracles for people in a hurting world.

As a small group or house church leader, you may sense a "stirring in your heart." Don't be afraid to express this to the others in the group. Sometimes that's all the encouragement needed in order for someone to step out in faith. Small group and house church members may give words of wisdom and knowledge to others in the group, and healing will flow.

If the Holy Spirit tells you to have a time of kneeling down in prayer, that is exactly what you should do. A deep prayer session may be the most moving and exciting thing your group may ever experience. To allow God to move will truly be the best thing your small group or house church can do. Always be sensitive to new people in the group. Explain to them in private from the Scriptures why you do certain things.

All in all, the small group or house church is a gathering God is using in the Christian's school of the Holy Spirit. Personal prophecies can be given with the understanding that "we prophesy in part" and that there are proper ways to process that type of a word from the Lord.

Sometimes it is wise if personal prophecies can be recorded or written down to be given to the local church leadership, pastor, or house church network leadership for confirmation. The Bible tells us to "test all things" and "do all things properly and in an orderly manner." It is best that personal prophecies not be given outside or in a corner somewhere without someone in leadership present. This will ensure proper spiritual protection to the person giving the personal prophecy as well as to the person receiving it. It will also help alleviate anyone being misled or improperly responding to the prophetic word that they have received.

If a small group or house church has a lack of experience in the gifts of the Holy Spirit, my suggestion would be to invite someone into the group who has a prophetic gift to equip the believers in this area. After a few weeks of equipping by a prophetic minister, the people in the group will find a new freedom to operate in the gifts of the Holy Spirit.

Find a Fit for New Believers

Since the small group in a cell-based church is the place for each believer to become actively involved in their church, each new person should be encouraged to become involved in a small group as soon as they can.

Ralph Neighbour Jr. says in *Where Do We Go From Here?*:

> As the cells grow, many small congregations will be formed. However, they do not replace the cells as the most significant part of church life. For example, no one ever joins a congregation; the only available link to its ministry is to join a cell.[4]

Several times during our first years as a church, we closed down our Sunday celebration meetings for a month. During this time, everyone met in homes in small groups on Sunday mornings. Not only does this strengthen the groups (the underground church), but it also does not give an option for believers to be involved in a Sunday morning celebration without becoming involved in the life of the church—the small group aspect of the church. These were often rewarding times. Several years ago when the Lord impressed on us to stop meeting in celebrations for one month and instead meet in homes on Sunday mornings, 100 people were added to small groups within the church.

The local pastor of a cell-based church may ask a small group leader to call or visit some of these new people to give them information about their group. If, for some reason, the newcomers do not feel at home in the small group that is recommended, the small group leader refers them back to the local pastor or other church leader who will continue to assist them. We encourage these new people to pray and ask the Lord where He wants them to serve.

Since DCFI started, we have felt impressed of the Lord to ask for two types of people to be added to His Church: pre-Christians and believers who are called by the Lord to labor with us in building His Church from house to house and reaching the pre-Christians. In other words, some of the people being directed to our small group or house church may already be Christians who need to be joined to a local church and others may be new believers from a totally unchurched background who may have had little or no Bible background.

In the small group and house church, the more mature Christians can quickly be trained to disciple younger ones in the Lord. This is God's plan for bringing His body to maturity. It's important that everyone is discipled and trained in the basics of the Christian life.

Understand What Your Group Believes

If a new believer wants to become a part of the small group or house church, he needs to know what they believe. Every local church and house church network should have a systematic way of sharing the Scriptures so individuals can understand exactly what they believe. Just as each family has a particular way of doing things, so each church family has various scriptural understandings and expectations. A church needs to be clear about what its members believe concerning important issues and biblical doctrines.

Most DCFI churches encourage newcomers to go through a "Biblical Foundation Series" to help believers understand basic biblical truths. The course currently consists of 12 teachings on DVDs that can be viewed on Sunday mornings at the celebration service, in the small group or house church setting during the week, or in an individual's home.

These 12 sessions help us understand who we are as a church and assist us in knowing what we believe. In many DCFI cell-based churches, anyone in a small group who has not taken the course is encouraged to do so before expressing commitment to the church in the small group. Viewing these videos periodically as a group, especially when new members come in, is an excellent way to help a new person get established in the small group. This training is also available for house churches.

These same Biblical Foundations are also accessible in a two-book series entitled *Discovering the Basic Truths of Christianity* and *Building Your Life on the Basic Truths of Christianity*.[5] They are often utilized by small group leaders and house churches to disciple new believers and familiarize those who are new to the church with the basic spiritual principles the Lord has given us as a church family.

In the same way that every family is unique and varied, each church family has its own set of family guidelines. Either a Biblical Foundation Course or a similar substitute will help new persons make a final decision concerning where the Lord may be placing them in the Body of Christ.

Dissolve a Stagnant Group

To maintain healthy small groups and house churches, the groups will eventually need to multiply. Sometimes this is easier said than done. People often tend to get comfortable in their group. We have had groups that were together for quite some time without multiplying, and they were satisfied with their experiences of mutual support, often forgetting their mission to reach out.

A problem with that is that the closer we look at our faces in the mirror each morning, the more imperfections we see. In the small group and house church setting, if we just sit around and look at each other and forget our mission to reach out, we can quickly begin to dwell on the imperfections that we see in one another. This will inevitably lead us down a road of disillusionment and decline.

When a small group or house church leader and others in the group sense they have become spiritually stagnant, with no one desiring to multiply another group from the parent one, they realize they may need to eventually dissolve or discontinue altogether. This is not always an easy task for the leader.

It is helpful to have the local pastor or the network leadership of a house church involved in the process of a small group or house church that dissolves. This is another reason why house churches should be connected to a network of other house churches, so that there are external godly leaders to help them to process these kinds of changes. Often a spiritual overseer that we are in relationship with will have the grace and experience to help the members to quickly find their place in another group before the enemy can sow seeds of discouragement and confusion into their lives.

Sometimes when a small group or house church dissolves, it takes a period of time for believers to get involved in another group. It can be helpful for the small group or house church leader to start a "transition group" that he leads temporarily to support God's people and help them discern their future small group involvement.

The Multiplication Process

The healthy process of multiplication in human cells is called "mitosis." It is multiplication by dividing. One cell becomes two, and each continues to grow until they, too, divide and separate to become four cells.

All small groups and house churches should eventually multiply. But they first go through different stages. Each small group and house church goes through a period of gestation (growth and learning) before it can give birth to a new group.

For a new small group or house church, the first few months is a good time for sharing testimonies and building new relationships. Everyone could explain how they came to the Lord, how they were filled with the Holy Spirit, and other life-changing experiences. It is very healthy to discuss these spiritual experiences. It is in this way that people begin to be knit together and understand more about each other. It also provides opportunities for deeper friendships to develop.

During the next few months there should be more of an emphasis on bringing others into the group. Talk with friends, neighbors, those at work, and loved ones about Jesus and how He has changed your life. Tell them what is going on—what God is doing in your small group or house church. Expect people to come to a place of faith in Jesus Christ.

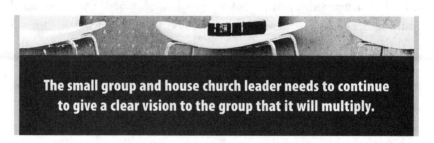

The small group and house church leader needs to continue to give a clear vision to the group that it will multiply.

The small group and house church leader needs to continue to give a clear vision to the group that it will multiply. Then, as the group gets larger, the people will begin to talk about birthing a new group. I was a member of one small group that became large and cumbersome. We decided to meet in smaller groups for prayer during our meetings. A month or two later we decided to take these four prayer groups and meet in separate homes. We were still a part of the same large group, but we met at times as smaller prayer meetings in different homes instead of always attending the regular small group meeting as often as we had before. After doing this for a while, some of the small prayer groups became so excited about their group that they decided to begin a new small group. It is said that some people never learn to swim until they jump into the water! The same is true with small group or house church multiplication.

Consequently, there should be a lot of prayer and open communication about specific upcoming changes. Give people some time to get used to a new idea until it is birthed in their own hearts and they welcome it. Then it will not be a traumatic thing, but something that people can look forward to with enthusiasm and faith. Encourage each person to seek the Lord's wisdom on any proposed change and get back to you with a response. It is best if the move can be confirmed by as many people as possible in the group. During this time the small group or house church leaders should be accountable to the local church leaders or the house church network overseers who will pray with them and assist them in any way possible.

Remember, growth is healthy. A healthy church is a growing church—numerically, by the adding of people to His Kingdom and in maturity, by growing closer to our Lord Jesus.

"How often should a group multiply?" is one of the questions that I am most often asked by pastors and small group and house church leaders. The answer depends upon what the Holy Spirit is saying to you and in which culture you are living.

In the North American culture, I believe it's feasible for believers in small groups and house churches to ask the Lord for the grace to spawn a new group or house church each year, although we would never make it a requirement. We have noticed that other cultures and nations usually multiply new groups much more often.

We tell our small groups or house churches that if they have the grace to multiply more often than once a year, they should do it. It's a wonderful goal to have, and goals are important, but they must be birthed by the Holy Spirit and be attainable. We must admit, some of the goals that we set in our early years as a church are embarrassing. We set a goal early on to be a church of 40,000 people during the first years we were in existence. In retrospect, this goal was based much more on a mathematical calculation than it was on a word from the Holy Spirit!

Another time, after a group from DCFI returned from our first visit to the then largest church in the world, in Seoul, Korea, we were all excited about quickly setting goals. Although the concept of goal setting was good and needed, we set goals that were not spiritually attainable for all of the small group leaders. We told the leaders that they needed to multiply their groups every six months, just like they did in Korea. This is certainly a good goal; however, each group and leader is at a different place spiritually. Although some groups enthusiastically trusted the Lord for their group to multiply every six months, other small group leaders began to "burn out" because of not being able to meet these expectations. Along with our leadership team, I asked their forgiveness for placing these stringent requirements on them.

We do believe, however, that to trust the Lord for at least two people or families to come to Christ through our small group or house church each year is certainly not setting a goal that is too high. Those who have no spirit-led goals often have no vision. And without a clear vision, the Scriptures tell us we will perish.

When it is time for a small group or house church to multiply, everyone will be ready for it because they were preparing for this process all along. Often a group has been praying for a particular town or area, and a few members who live there subsequently feel called to begin a new small group or house church in that town. Because assistant leaders have been raised up previously in the group, there is always ongoing leadership potential to accommodate multiplication.

And remember, the purpose for multiplication in the small group or house church is to see God's people released to train others and fulfill God's Word (see 2 Tim. 2:2), not just to meet a goal. The early believers walked in the fear of the Lord and in the comfort of the Holy Spirit and were multiplied (see Acts 9:31). We are called to do the same.

One small group that was multiplying invited all of the other small groups in their city to celebrate the "small group multiplication" at a local restaurant. Nearly everyone came from the groups in the entire city. It was a festive occasion. There was a time of rejoicing that the Lord had given the group the opportunity to multiply into two. There was a time of prayer for the new and original small group leaders. Soon after the multiplication took place, the new group doubled in size and the original group became nearly as large as it was previously.

The natural tendency is for believers in the small groups or house churches to want to stay together. However, if we can understand our Lord's heart to see new people come into His Kingdom, multiplication will be a great joy as the Kingdom of God continues to grow through our small groups and house churches.

Small groups and house churches are not immune to problems. In the next chapter, we will take a look at some problems that may occur and give leaders possible solutions.

QUESTIONS TO THINK ABOUT
From Chapter 12

1. Contrast being "unprepared" with being "led by the Holy Spirit."

2. How can a small group encourage members to step out in faith and practice spiritual gifts?

3. Why is it better to use the term "multiply" rather than "split" or "divide"?

CHAPTER 13

Help! I'm a Leader

All of us experience times of crisis. This is an opportune time for the small group or house church to get actively involved in practical ministry. If you are a small group or house church leader and someone in your group is going through a crisis, you should activate the members of your group to serve the person as you see appropriate.

When a storm brought a huge tree crashing down on their house roof, one family experienced God's love in action through their small group. "Love started flowing our way the very next day in the form of a tub of brownies from a member," they reported. "Brownies don't solve a mess, but they sure lift your spirits!" Small group members came immediately to remove the tree from the roof. One evening everyone from the group helped to repair water damage to the inside of the house. They hung a drop ceiling, painted, fixed a door, and did electrical work and many other smaller jobs. This family's misfortune was turned to a blessing as members had the opportunity to "do it unto Jesus" as they helped bear each other's burdens.

During times of crisis or change in someone's life, it's important to respond with an attitude of love, gentleness, and compassion. A storm-torn house, change of jobs, the death of a loved one, moving, and the birth of a baby are all types of change that add extra pressures to our lives.

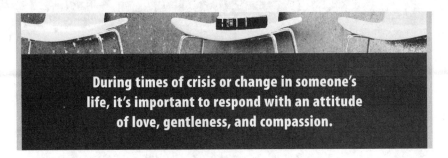

During times of crisis or change in someone's life, it's important to respond with an attitude of love, gentleness, and compassion.

Remember, faith works by love. As you identify with the person's situation, God will show you how to best respond. The Lord has called us to all work together to build the Body of Christ.

Practical Tips

Here are a few examples of what you can do when someone in your group is going through the following crisis or change:

- **Hospitalization**—provide prayer, visitation, calls to family, flowers, child care, or house-sitting. Contact the local pastor or house church network overseer to let him know of the hospitalization, especially in the case of an extended or serious illness.

- **Illness**—If a person is absent from the small group or house church meeting due to illness, the entire group should be encouraged to be involved in prayer for the sick, visiting, taking meals to the family, providing transportation, and sending cards and flowers.

- **Financial need**—If someone has a financial or material need, you may want to initiate a special offering to help meet the need. If it is greater than the group can meet, the need should be discussed with your local pastor or house church network overseer. As I mentioned before, many local DCFI congregations have a "deacon's fund." This fund receives a percentage of the monies that are given to the church through the weekly tithes as well as special designated offerings. All monies that are in the deacon's fund are set apart to help those who have special financial needs, and these funds are administered through the small group, which provides a sense of accountability.

- **Moving**—When someone moves, the leader sets the standard as a servant and gives leadership to the others within the small group or house church who are assisting in the moving of a family or a single person from one location to another. Encourage the group to assist with packing, moving, child care, and meals. It can be a great time of fellowship for your group! The responsibility for organizing the moving day, including helping to line up trucks, should be delegated to others within the small group or house church as much as is possible; however, the leader should take the responsibility to make sure that it happens.

- **Death in the family**—Be sensitive to the needs of the family. Pray for them and serve wherever you can. Local pastors and house church network overseers will serve with the leader during these times of crisis. Due to the leader's close relationship with the family that has experienced a death, he may receive the information before the pastor or overseer. If this happens, leaders are encouraged to contact their spiritual overseers immediately. They should ask the pastor or overseer how the group can effectively undergird the family during this time.

- **New baby**—Set up a schedule to provide meals for the family. Perhaps you can baby-sit some of the other children in the family during this time and set up a schedule for others within the group to serve in this way. Again, in a cell-based church, the small group leader may find out about the new baby before the local pastor receives the information. We encourage the small group leader in a cell-based church to be sure to contact the local pastor with this information immediately.

- **Person with a life-controlling problem**—You may want to contact your local pastor or house church network overseer for assistance and training for a particular problem. Each of us is an able minister of the new covenant and can be used of the Lord to minister His healing; however, there are times when the Lord may want to use someone else within the Body of Christ who has a special anointing in an area of healing. There also may be a special need for emotional healing or deliverance.

Delegate, Delegate, Delegate

Many small group or house church leaders find it hard to delegate and then end up doing most of the work themselves. There are two major problems with not delegating to others. First of all, leaders who do not delegate sometimes get overwhelmed with their responsibilities. And second, if the leader does everything himself, the others in the group miss out on the blessing of serving, learning new responsibilities, and exercising their spiritual gifts.

Sometimes small group and house church leaders tend to do things themselves because of past experiences of being turned down when they asked others to fulfill a certain responsibility. Or perhaps the person the responsibility was delegated to did his job so poorly that the leader spent more time cleaning up the mess than if he would have done the whole thing himself. But if we do not give others responsibilities, how will they ever have the opportunity to learn?

Before we delegate a certain responsibility to a member, we need to be sure that we have trained them in this responsibility. Don't take it for granted that they know what to do. They may need coaching. For example, if you ask a member to care for the children, be sure that he knows what is expected of him. Otherwise you will abdicate instead of delegate. Abdication sows seeds of frustration for everyone.

Remember, delegate everything that you possibly can. Work yourself out of a job. As others increase in responsibility, you can begin to decrease and move on to the next thing the Lord has for you to do.

Dealing With Difficult Problems

Small group and house church leadership is not an easy responsibility, but it is rewarding. When someone in a small group or house church has problems the leader feels are too intense for him to handle, we encourage him to contact his local pastor or house church network overseer. They can deal with the situation and the small group leader or house church leader remains available to follow through with any assistance that may be needed.

For example, if Bob has a need that is greater than the small group leader in a cell-based church has faith to handle, the local pastor is there, as one who has grace from the Lord to serve the small group leader and Bob.

Bob, of course, is free to go to *anyone* for advice, counsel, prayer, and fellowship if he feels so led. During our early years we made the mistake of exercising too much control and not enough flexibility in this area. For example, if Bob had a problem or struggle, we strongly suggested that he talk to the small group leader first before talking to anyone else. Although this was, generally speaking, a good principle to follow, the legalistic manner in which it was carried out was unduly constraining.

Sometimes a person needs to share confidential information but has not yet built enough trust in his relationship with the small group or house church leader or another person in the group. Trust takes time. The ideal situation is for every member to have a close enough relationship with other believers in their small group or house church so they can discuss anything, but that is not always the case.

We encourage people within the church to be free to go to anyone they feel they need to go to. Sometimes this may be a professional counselor within or outside their church. Usually if the problem they are facing requires accountability, they will eventually be encouraged to open up their hearts to their small group leader, house church leader, or local pastor. Of course, a trust relationship must be established before they will feel comfortable doing this.

Next to prayer, the person experiencing the difficulty needs a friend. As the leader, take this opportunity to befriend the one in trouble, building a deeper relationship with that person.

Problems in the area of alcohol, drugs, physical abuse, finances, health, and so on may require a counselor who can relate to those areas specifically. Pastors and counselors who have been delivered from a particular bondage often are called to minister to others with that same problem. The house church network leader or local pastors help put the leader in touch with the appropriate person.

When helping someone work through a difficulty, we believe it is important to never counsel the opposite sex alone. As much as possible, men should counsel men and women counsel women. If it is necessary to counsel someone of the opposite sex, always have a third party present. This will avert temptation, the appearance of evil, or any opportunity for gossip or false accusations.

Emotional Dependency

There may be times when we find that certain persons who are in the group are constantly draining us of our time and energy in a way that is not best for them or us. This is often called emotional dependency.[1]

Sometimes due to the past patterns that we developed before knowing Christ, or due to our family of origin or possibly even from some wrong spiritual teaching, we develop the dysfunctional pattern of using others to meet our needs. Everyone desires to be loved and valued. Often, we overstep our boundaries when we attempt to meet those needs solely through others or when others desire the same from us.

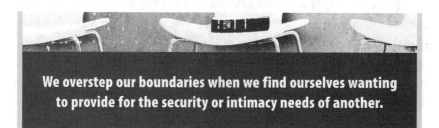

We overstep our boundaries when we find ourselves wanting to provide for the security or intimacy needs of another.

You may find a person attracted to your small group or house church or to you as a leader because the basic needs of love and acceptance, security, and intimacy are unmet in his life. These are legitimate needs, and while it is true that the group can provide love, support, and acceptance, it is not appropriate that the small group, house church, or the leader become the sole source to meet these needs. The natural outgrowth of relationships developing within the small group or house church will provide for some emotional needs but can never replace the natural family, parents, or a spouse. While the small group provides support, it is not a "support group" like Alcoholic Anonymous. We overstep our boundaries when we find ourselves wanting to provide for the security or intimacy needs of another.

Let me share an example that I believe exhibited emotional dependency. Sally started coming to one of our small groups with her two children. In the very first meeting, Sally began manipulating the group by sharing her needs about her truck-driving husband. Apparently he was gone most of the week and left Sally to run the household. Her children were totally out of control (starved for consistent godly discipline, you might say), and it was obvious that Sally was not looking to give anything to the group, but rather, to receive from it. In time, we discovered that she needed baby-sitters, help with her marriage, and help with their finances. She began to spend hours of time with various women in the small group, usually by unannounced "drop-ins." Sally did not show a desire to come closer to Jesus or be discipled. What she did desire was to have the uncomfortable things in her life "fixed" by the caretakers and responsible ones within the group. Sally wanted to be rescued and cared for.

The truth is that we could give and give to Sally and her family (which we initially attempted to do), but nothing or no one could fill the emotional void in her life. Recognizing this from the beginning could have spared many well-meaning people from becoming burned out.

Then what do we do with verses such as Luke 6:38, "Give and it shall be given" and Matthew 10:8, "Freely you have received, freely give..."? Here are some questions you can ask yourself. These same questions could be applied to help the one displaying emotionally dependent behavior.

- Am I in relation with this person or is this person in relation with me or the small group or house church as an approval-seeker?

- Do I feel overly responsible for this person? Is it Christ-given compassion, or is it guilt-filled sympathy?

- When I'm around this person, do I feel as though he or she is looking to me to provide for his or her need of security and relational intimacy?

- Am I, or is this person, looking to this relationship for identity?

To the woman at the well, Jesus truthfully responded, *"You are right when you say you have no husband. The fact is, you have had five husbands, and the man you now have is not your husband"* (John 4:17-18). Jesus did not become this woman's emotional rescuer. He let her know that He knew her lifestyle and situation. In verse 26, He then revealed to her, *"...I who speak to you am He* [the Messiah]."

To the man at the pool of Bethesda, an invalid for 38 years, perhaps quite dependent upon his condition and surroundings, He asked:

"...Do you want to be made well?" (John 5:6).

Remember, we are not the Savior. We do not need to meet needs or find needs in order to be important in the Kingdom. We are important to Jesus before we *do* anything. The newborn baby does not meet needs; it only has needs, yet the parent loves, accepts, and approves of that child. In the same way, God loves and approves of us. Rather than forming dependent relationships with one another, we need to look to Jesus and lead others to look to Him also.

Codependency

Codependency is not to be confused with emotional dependency, and the terms should not be interchangeably used. Whereas emotional dependency has to do with placing any human relationship before our relationship with God (which is idolatry), codependency relates more to our need to help, fix, enable, or control someone with a life-controlling need.

Why is the topic of codependency and small group and house church leadership so important? Leanne Payne, in her book *Restoring the Christian Soul Through Healing Prayer,* wrote that Christians in their zeal to serve others may actually mistake humility for idolatry by enabling sick and sinful behavior in the ones they are serving.[2]

Plainly and simply, small group and house church leaders desire their members to be whole spiritually, physically, and emotionally. When they are not whole, there can be a strong tendency to become the "caretaker."

Let's define what we mean by codependency. Early on, the term codependency related to the spouse, child, or some significant person who was closely involved in the family system of one who was chemically dependent. For example: If mom is addicted to prescription drugs, it will undoubtedly affect the whole family. It will affect the finances, the marriage relationship, and the relationship with the children. Mom will have good days and bad days. She may forget appointments. Mother becomes the dependent one, while the remainder of the family becomes codependent.

Today, the term has evolved to mean something far beyond this definition. However, for the scope of this book, we will be dealing with the issues of "care-taking" or "over-responsibility" within the small group and house church.

Small group or house church leaders are often confronted with people in need. Let's say that the Broad Street group has been reaching out to the Johns family. Mr. Johns is an alcoholic. He spends his paycheck on alcohol, and Mrs. Johns must pay all the household bills and feed her family of five on $100 per week. Consequently, she often finds herself in need of help.

Mrs. Johns shares her needs with the group but has a tendency to cover up her husband's drinking. Perhaps she even blames the problem on her husband's low-paying job. Of course the group wants to help. The children need food, and Mrs. Johns needs to be delivered of all the financial pressure. It certainly seems right to help in whatever way necessary.

Codependency causes us to lose our objectivity and take on a warped sense of responsibility. How long can the Broad Street group help? Perhaps to answer this question, we should ask another. How long can Mr. Johns be an alcoholic?

Mr. Johns' addiction is controlling his family. His wife wants to be rescued, helped, fixed. But, enabling this family to function normally while Mr. Johns remains addicted is very unhealthy. By *enabling,* I mean being involved in behavior that helps to relieve the pain of the consequences of addiction. Relieving pain, however, may not be helping anyone.

When small group leaders, house church leaders, or members begin desiring their worth from what they do for others, they are displaying characteristics of codependency. No matter how much is done, it will never be enough. That guilt will still be there. Their attempts to please others are designed to win approval and acceptance.

How then do we help the Johns family? Perhaps we can start with the practical, immediate needs of food, finances, and other needs. But these things are not the ongoing need. Mr. Johns needs Jesus and lots of healing. Until he comes to Christ, Mrs. Johns really needs to be confronted with the truth. Her covering up for Mr. Johns is codependent behavior. She needs to be honest with herself, her feelings, her children, her small group or house church, and her husband. Denial never changes a thing.

And for small group leaders, house church leaders, or members who have a tendency to enable and rescue, an identity in Christ is the answer. Such Scriptures as Romans 8:1,17,33,35-39; Ephesians 1:22; Colossians 3:12; and many others describe who we are in Christ.[3]

Maintaining proper beliefs as discussed in the emotional dependency section is very important. As long as the group helps around the Johns' house, clothes the children, and pays the overdue bills, Mr. Johns can continue in his addiction, and Mrs. Johns will never have to face the truth. As *Focus on the Family* founder, Dr. James Dobson, appropriately says, "At times, love must be tough."[4]

Divisiveness in the Small Group or House Church

Paul the Apostle gives us a strong admonition regarding those who are divisive in the church:

> But avoid foolish disputes, genealogies, contentions, and strivings about the law; for they are unprofitable and useless. Reject a divisive man after the first and second admonition, knowing that such a person is warped and sinning, being self-condemned (Titus 3:9-11).

A divisive spirit can do more harm in a church than anything else that I can think of. It is usually cloaked with super-spiritual terminology like, "Do you really think our small group or house church leader or our pastor is anointed by the Lord to give the type of leadership that we need?" A divisive spirit will creep into a small group or a house church like cancer. That is why Paul speaks so harshly about it.

If you are a small group or house church leader and someone in the group is being divisive, don't waste any time. Go to him in love and confront the situation. God hates division, and we need to hate it as much as He does. Show him what the Scriptures say about being divisive.

Some time ago, when I pastored the original DCFI church, one of the men in the church began to sow seeds of discontent. He was giving his opinion about how he differed with some of the decisions that the church leadership was making. It was done in a way that was not constructive. Some of the Lord's people were confused. His actions were also causing strain on our relationship. When I realized what was happening, I faced my fears of confrontation and sat down with this brother in Christ and told him what I was seeing. He received my admonition, and today our relationship is restored.

Church Discipline

In First Corinthians 5 and Matthew 18:15-20, there are explicit instructions for dealing with serious problems in the church. People must be confronted with their sins, but always in the compassionate love of Christ. If Tom, a fellow small group or house church member, is overcome by a sin, we should first pray for him and allow the Spirit of God to give us a heart of genuine compassion for him. According to Matthew 18, we should talk with him alone about how he has disobeyed God. If he does not receive us, then we should take someone with us and talk to him again. This could be someone in the small group or house church, a local pastor or spiritual overseer, or another Christian friend.

At this point, if Tom does not receive the admonition of the local church, the Scripture tells us that we should not consider him as a believer in Jesus Christ. If we get to this last step with Tom and he does not turn from his sin, a local pastor or house church network overseer should be involved in helping to deal with the situation.

We believe this type of scriptural church discipline is most effectively handled in a small group setting. We are instructed in Matthew 18 and in First Corinthians 5 to take these matters to the church. The church that meets in the home provides the proper spiritual setting. In the group, there is a deep sense of love and compassion for Tom, because we know him.

If Tom repents, it will be a great joy for the small group or house church to see Tom come back into a proper relationship with the Lord. The goal of all discipline is future restoration. Restoration will only be effective if done in a spirit of gentleness. God calls Christian leaders, as servant leaders, to restore someone, not by domineering, but by sharing the truth in love.

> Brothers, if someone is caught in a sin, you who are spiritual should restore him gently. But watch yourself, or you also may be tempted (Galatians 6:1).

The local pastors and house church network overseers have special grace on their lives to help small group or house church leaders handle church discipline situations in a godly, compassionate way.

Vows of Confidentiality

As leaders, there have been times in the past when we have fallen into the trap of promising to not divulge information that was given to us in confidence, when in reality, it would have been much better for everyone involved to share this information with others. The Scriptures tell us in Proverbs 6:2:

> ...*you have been trapped by what you said, ensnared by the words of your mouth.*

If Bill tells us personal information and asks us to promise not to tell anyone, our response must be, "I will only do what is the most loving thing that I can do for you and for anyone else involved, and what is best for the Lord's Kingdom." If Bill doesn't trust me enough to allow me to get help for him when he needs it, it is best for him not to divulge personal information. Basic confidentiality is important, but vows of confidentiality should be avoided.

Taking this approach will keep you from being ensnared by the words of your mouth. In other words, you will not be stuck with private information that you know you should tell others who could be a part of the solution but feel unable to discuss because of a promise of confidentiality.

Now that you've been given some advice on how to deal with potential problem areas in the small group and house church, in the next chapter I want to concentrate on every small group and house church leader's commitment to Jesus Christ, to those he serves, to his local church or house church network's vision, and on his commitment to flexibility so that the small group or house church may flow together in unity.

QUESTIONS TO THINK ABOUT
From Chapter 13

1. List some practical ways that small groups and house churches can help members.

2. How do you handle one who gossips against a leader?

3. What are the steps to restore someone back into fellowship?

CHAPTER 14

A Leader's Commitment

If anyone would come after Me, he must deny himself and take up his cross and follow Me (Matthew 16:24).

If you hold to My teaching, you are really My disciples. Then you will know the truth, and the truth will set you free (John 8:31-32).

I have hidden Your word in my heart that I might not sin against You (Psalm 119:11).

First and foremost, our commitment must be total surrender to Jesus Christ as Lord and Master and living a life in accordance to the Word of God. There can be no compromise. The Church is built on Jesus

Christ. Although our relationships and plans to reach those who do not yet believe Jesus, along with encouraging believers to be knit together in cell groups and house churches, are important, they are secondary to our relationship with Jesus.

Commitment to the Local Church and the Body of Christ

Those who accepted his message were baptized, and about three thousand were added to their number that day. They devoted themselves to the apostles' teaching and to the fellowship, to the breaking of bread and to prayer (Acts 2:41-42).

The church is people in relationship with God and with each other, within the framework of a local expression of the Body of Christ. It is not commitment to a building made of bricks and mortar. To be committed to our local Body literally means we are willing to be totally sold out to Jesus and to be an active participant with other believers in a specific small group or house church.

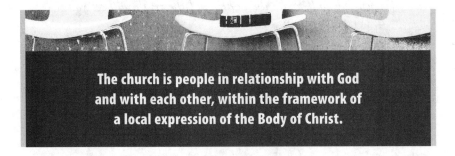

The church is people in relationship with God and with each other, within the framework of a local expression of the Body of Christ.

The small group or house church leader's life is an example to other members on how to be actively involved in the lives of people. This includes showing an interest in the people and getting together with them on occasions other than the small group or house church meeting. Meetings are great, but real community usually happens outside the meetings. Any leader who depends only on meetings to minister and build relationships with the people in his group is destined for failure.

People are looking for reality. Real life is not confined to meetings. It happens as we work together, play tennis together, pray together, fix the car together, bake cookies together, witness together, and eat together. The list of things we can do together is endless. This is the stuff real church is made of.

Commitment to the Vision of the Church

Jesus had a personal vision. Therefore, He endured the cross. "Let us fix our eyes on Jesus, the author and perfecter of our faith, who for the joy set before Him endured the cross, scorning its shame, and sat down at the right hand of the throne of God" (Hebrews 12:2).

Every business, every family, every person, every church should have a vision. Just as those who are married verbalize their commitment to their spouse by saying, "I love you," we need to verbalize our commitment to support the vision that the Lord has given to us as a local church.

We must caution, however: exalting our church's vision above Jesus will lead to idolatry. God is the ultimate visionary, and we are created in His image. We are given the potential to dream and have visions. If we shift our primary focus from Jesus to our vision, we'll become ensnared.

Many times during the past years I have had to refocus my vision and energies to my relationship with Jesus first and then to the vision that the Lord has given to us as a church and a church movement. John the Apostle tells us in First John 5:21, *"Dear children, keep yourselves from idols."* Idolatry can be so subtle that we can be ensnared by it before we know what has happened. When we begin to emphasize the vision that the Lord has given to us more than we emphasize our relationship with Jesus, we create an idol in our hearts. Ezekiel the prophet tells us, *"Son of man, these men have set up idols in their hearts and put wicked stumbling blocks before their faces…"* (Ezek. 14:3).

Even a God-inspired vision, when given preeminence above the Lord Himself, will cause us to stumble. One of the dangers of having a good small group or house church structure is that we can begin to trust the structure more than the Holy Spirit. Jesus will share His glory with no other. It can be so subtle, but a small group or house church vision, even though it has been birthed by the Holy Spirit, can divert us from a simple love for and devotion to Jesus. We have learned through experience that focusing on the vision and structure more than focusing on Jesus produces spiritual barrenness. Only a relationship with Jesus produces life. We must stay tender before the Lord and fellowship with Him.

It is important for the small group and house church leader to understand and articulate the vision of the local church or house church network and then discuss it with their group regularly. It has been said that every church must have a compelling vision (a clear call from God), a defined mission (what is our purpose), and a well laid-out plan (how are we going to do it).

The vision and mission that the Lord has given to DOVE Christian Fellowship International has been written down in the form of a vision statement, a mission statement, and a plan in the form of 12 values. (See Appendix B at the end of the book for DCFI's statements.)

Commitment to Goals

A goal is a statement of faith, a course of action. Jesus is returning to this earth. It is a goal that He has fixed. God has goals for His Body and for each of us individually. We, like the apostle Paul, must run toward those goals that God has set before us.

> *I press on toward the goal to win the prize for which God has called me heavenward in Christ Jesus* (Philippians 3:14).

Therefore I do not run like a man running aimlessly; I do not fight like a man beating the air (1 Corinthians 9:26).

Every small group and house church needs clear, attainable goals. It's also essential for each small group and house church leader to have clear goals. Ask the Lord what goals He wants you to set for yourself as a leader. God's plan is to use each of us to set goals under the Holy Spirit's direction to change the world in which we live. Godly goals cause us to become intentional about obeying the Lord.

If you have a goal to pray for each member of your group every day, don't just say you will pray every day. Set a specific goal that is clear, measurable, and attainable. For example, decide to pray one minute a day for each person and progress from there.

As you set goals as a group, try to involve as many persons in the small group or house church as possible in the process. This way the whole group will feel a sense of responsibility for these goals to be reached. If you implement new goals and ideas too fast, the group may feel lost.

I grew up as a farm boy. During the fall of every year we dug our sweet potatoes for the winter. We placed these sweet potatoes in baskets and put them on a truck. Then came the excitement of driving the farm truck filled with sweet potatoes from the field to the house. Driving that old pick-up truck was a real art. We had to round the corners very slowly or we would upset the whole load of sweet potatoes. In the same way, when we make spiritual decisions that will affect others, we need to give them enough time to know that they are a part of the decision-making process so that they don't "fall off the truck." Discuss new ideas with those in your group before making final decisions. You are called as a team to see the Kingdom of God built together.

Get away to pray, so the goals you set are not natural goals, but goals that are birthed by the Holy Spirit. Maybe the Lord will make it clear to you that you should trust Him to see a family receive Christ within the next two months. Or perhaps you will have as a goal to spend a certain amount of time together in prayer each week. Ask the Lord for a practical goal regarding your group's multiplication. There is an old saying, "If you fail to plan, you plan to fail!"

May I interject a word of caution concerning goals? To not reach your goal may not necessarily be failure. On the other hand, to reach your goal may not be success. Ministry to the Lord and to people must be the ultimate goal!

Commitment to Be Willing to Change

The only thing that is constant on this earth is the Word of God and change. It is a bit unnerving, but true. As we truly follow the leading of the Holy Spirit, we will continue to change. *"The wind blows where it wishes, and you hear the sound of it, but cannot tell where it comes from and where it goes. So is everyone who is born of the Spirit"* (John 3:8).

Our small groups and house churches will change, and each of us will continue to change as we mature in Christ. Our ways of thinking must also change.

Years ago, during the early days of my involvement in a para-church youth ministry, the young people giving their lives to Jesus wanted to be baptized in water as new believers. Back then, most people seemed to be under the impression that only the pastor or bishop of a church could perform baptisms. So we had to look high and low to find a pastor who was willing to baptize these new believers despite the fact that they were not yet ready to become members of his congregation. We found ourselves swimming upstream, cutting across the Christian culture of our community. Although today it has become more acceptable for all believers to share in the work of the church and participate in baptisms, those who build according to an underground pattern in small groups and house churches still find themselves going against the flow. However, if the Lord tarries, the church may look different several years from now. We should not be afraid of change.

Change is hard for most of us. But if we are going to grow and mature, we must constantly be ready to embrace change. For example, the change that takes place when a small group or house church multiplies is not easy for many of us. And as leaders, we must help others get ready for the change. It often helps God's people when they realize that even leaders do not necessarily feel like changing, but they understand that change is a part of normal church life.

We are naturally resistant to change. Human nature has always resisted change. A case in point is the following letter written by Martin Van Buren, then governor of New York, to President Jackson, concerning an "evil" new business enterprise threatening our nation:

January 31, 1829

To President Jackson,

The canal system of this country is being threatened by the spread of a new form of transportation known as "railroads." The federal government must preserve the canals for the following reasons:

1. If canal boats are supplanted by "railroads," serious unemployment will result. Captains, cooks, drivers, hostlers, repairmen and lock tenders will be left without means of livelihood, not to mention the numerous farmers now employed in growing hay for the horses.

2. Boat builders would suffer, and towline, whip and harness makers would be left destitute.

3. Canal boats are absolutely essential to defend the United States. In the event of the expected trouble with England, the Erie Canal would be the only means by which we could ever move the supplies so vital to waging modern war.

As you may well know, Mr. President, "railroad" car-
riages are pulled at the enormous speed of fifteen miles
per hour by "engines" which, in addition to endanger-
ing life and limb of passengers, roar and snort their way
through the countryside, setting fire to crops, scaring
the livestock and frightening women and children. The
Almighty certainly never intended that people should
travel at such breakneck speed.

—*Martin Van Buren, Governor of New York.*[1]

It's amazing and even amusing that a future president of the United
States was extremely resistant to a change that was inevitable. Nothing
would stop the change that was on the horizon. It is also inevitable that
the Lord has "change" in store for His Church, and nothing will stop the
change that is coming in the future.

Building the church through small groups and house churches requires
a lot of flexibility and change. But then, that is what life is all about. One
of my friends from YWAM told me one time, "Either we can keep everything neat and organized, or we can continue to allow the Lord to birth
new things among us. Birthing is messy and painful, but there is life!" I
vote for life. How about you?

As believers minister in practical ways (laying hands on the sick,
casting out demons, leading people to Christ, and serving people as the
opportunities arise), we must be open to change. Seeing others come to
Jesus and helping people step by step in their Christian walk—that's real
life! And it happens so effectively in the small group and house church
setting. The power of God is released as small groups of believers learn to
do the work of the Kingdom and stay open to change.

Commitment to the Group

Every local church has its own criteria regarding membership. I have often been asked the question, "What must I do to become a member of DOVE Christian Fellowship International?" Here is what we understand the Bible to say about being a member of the local church.

> *The body is a unit, though it is made up of many parts; and though all its parts are many, they form one body. So it is with Christ* (1 Corinthians 12:12).

The Church is called a "body" because everyone is connected somehow to everyone else and together they comprise a single unit. The finger cannot say, "I don't want to be attached to the hand." If it were disconnected, it would no longer have life flowing into it! This would also cause the entire hand to be at a disadvantage because the finger that belongs there is missing.

Membership in the early church was not membership in a club or participation in a meeting. It was practical commitment to Jesus Christ and to individual believers. We believe God wants to bring people into a spiritual family, not merely a weekly service. If a person begins to attend our Sunday morning celebrations in one of our cell-based churches but does not show any real interest in small group life, we remind him that, for us, commitment to the Body of Christ is not having one's name on a church roll. It is a commitment to be accountable in our Christian walk to a specific group of brothers and sisters in Christ as part of a small group or house church. Attending a Sunday morning service alone limits this person from experiencing the whole scope and thrust of our vision. Church leaders are encouraged to do whatever they can to help a believer find where the Lord is placing him in the Body of Christ. (Perhaps it will be in another church in our community.) Of course, this person may continue to attend our Sunday celebrations; he will not, however, be able to be involved in any area of leadership in the church until he is committed to a small group or house church.

Experiencing church in a small group setting has been wonderful for our family. Although it has been several years since I have had the privilege of serving as a small group leader (because of my travel schedule), my family and I are involved in a house church in our own community.

What a tremendous joy it has been for our family to serve and be served in a small group setting. We really experience church as a small group of believers. When our then 7-year-old son Josh desired to be baptized in water, I phoned our small group leader and the whole group went to a local indoor swimming pool where our leader and I baptized Josh. "Church" happened right there at the pool!

"What about a missionary or someone who has a job that would keep him away from the small group or house church meetings?" you may ask. "How can a person like this be committed to a small group or house church if he or she cannot attend the meetings?" The answer is simple. The meetings are not the issue. The issue is whether this believer wants to be connected in a living relationship with the other believers in this group.

When a young person graduates and goes to college, he is still a vital part of his natural family, although he does not sit down with them at the dinner table every night. The same principle applies to spiritual families in small groups and in house churches. There are other ways to keep in contact with a person apart from meeting in a formal setting. Phone calls and letters and text messages keep you close to someone who is far away geographically, whether for a short time or longer. Early morning breakfasts and many other get-togethers are possible with someone whose job makes it impossible to meet when the rest of the group normally gets together.

Commitment Card—A Tangible Way to Show Commitment

When I served as a senior pastor, we encouraged each person who became a part of a small group in our church to make a commitment to the others in that small group. This was not a commitment for a lifetime. It was a commitment for the duration of their time in their present small group. This was a scripturally based commitment that a person in any small group, house church, or other local church should be able to express with conviction and confidence to the others in their church.

A card was given to each person in the group listing the points of commitment to be expressed. Typically at the start of a new small group or when a new member joined, the entire small group used this card to profess their commitment to each other. This was not seen as a legalism, but as a privilege.

The commitment card stated:

> I confess Jesus Christ as Lord. I am therefore committed to living in obedience to the Word of God and the Holy Spirit, and to being part of the church that Jesus is building throughout the world. I specifically commit myself to the Body of Christ here at DOVE. I will be accountable to my brothers and sisters in the way I live my Christian life, and will support the leadership that God raises up and the vision God gives His Body.

A commitment like this or one similar can be printed on a card and used in your local church setting. Our commitment is to Jesus and His Word, to His Body at large, and to the local expression of the Body of Christ that the Lord has placed us in. Every local church (whether it is a cell-based church, house church, or traditional church) has four basic characteristics.

1. Each person has a relationship with God through Jesus Christ.

2. Each person has a relationship with others in their local church.

3. There is clear leadership recognized among the people.

4. There is a common vision.

We believe that these four characteristics are a proper assessment of the local church. We are not only committed to Jesus and the church universally, but also to the leadership and the specific vision that the Lord has given to a local body. This can be expressed and lived out practically in a small group or house church.

> *Now we ask you, brothers, to respect those who work hard among you, who are over you in the Lord and who admonish you. Hold them in the highest regard in love because of their work. Live in peace with each other* (1 Thessalonians 5:12-13).

> *Obey your leaders and submit to their authority. They keep watch over you as men who must give an account. Obey them so that their work will be a joy, not a burden, for that would be of no advantage to you* (Hebrews 13:17).

Building Unity

The Scriptures place a high priority on unity.

> *How good and pleasant it is when brothers live together in unity!* (Psalm 133:1)

> *I appeal to you, brothers, in the name of our Lord Jesus Christ, that all of you agree with one another so that there may be no divisions among you and that you may be perfectly united in mind and thought* (1 Corinthians 1:10).

> *...bearing with one another in love. Make every effort*

to keep the unity of the Spirit through the bond of peace
(Ephesians 4:2-3).

*There is one body and one Spirit—just as you were called
to one hope when you were called—one Lord, one faith,
one baptism; one God and Father of all, who is over all and
through all and in all* (Ephesians 4:4-6).

When the people in a small group or house church work together and flow with the Holy Spirit, there is unity and single-mindedness of purpose. As the small group leaders, house church leaders and other church leaders walk together in unity, the entire church is in unity together. As the leadership of one local church works in unity with the other local church leaders, the entire Body of Christ in that locality experiences a bond of unity together. That is when God commands a blessing!

It has often been said that prayer and unity are the two main ingredients for revival. The small group and house church leader will set the pace for unity and prayer in the group where he serves. If the leader is not in unity with the other leadership of the local church or house church network, he should not be in leadership of a small group or house church.

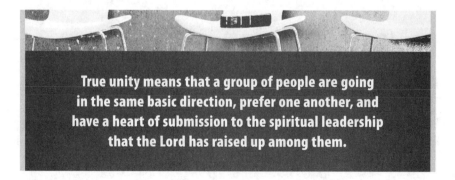

**True unity means that a group of people are going
in the same basic direction, prefer one another, and
have a heart of submission to the spiritual leadership
that the Lord has raised up among them.**

It is good to remember that unity does not mean everyone agrees on everything. I have never met two people who totally agree on everything.

However, true unity means that a group of people are going in the same basic direction, prefer one another, and have a heart of submission to the spiritual leadership that the Lord has raised up among them.

How did God raise up spiritual leadership in the New Testament church? In the next chapter, we will take a look at two groups of leaders who gave oversight and served the early church—apostles and elders.

QUESTIONS TO THINK ABOUT
From Chapter 14

1. What is your local church's vision and mission?

2. How can you help to implement this vision? Change is healthy. In what ways do you resist change?

3. How are you committed to your small group or house church?

PART
III

GOD POSITIONS US
FOR THE FUTURE

CHAPTER 15

New Testament Church Leadership Roles

I n order for the Church to be built from house to house according to an underground pattern, we need to take a fresh look at the Scriptures for a clearer understanding about church leadership. For example, since it has been so widely accepted throughout the world that the normal way to build the church is to find a pastor, a building, and to start filling the pews, this philosophy has also influenced our understanding of church leadership.

Apostles and Elders

When we study the Scriptures and look closely at the New Testament, we do not see a pastor-building mentality. Instead, we see two basic groups of governmental leaders who oversee and serve the churches who meet in homes and gather together corporately at the temple, or the school of Tyrannus (see Acts 19:9), or wherever else they can find to meet. Apostles and elders comprised these two groups of leaders found in Acts 15:4:

*And when they had come to Jerusalem, they were received by the church and the **apostles and the elders;** and they reported all things that God had done with them.*

Paul and Barnabas were having some problems with Jewish converts who were placing restrictions on the Gentile believers. Paul and Barnabas were convinced that these teachers from Judea were teaching a doctrine that was not according to faith, and that it would greatly hinder the work of God. So Paul and Barnabas went up to Jerusalem.

*This brought Paul and Barnabas into sharp dispute and debate with them. So Paul and Barnabas were appointed, along with some other believers, to go up to Jerusalem to see the **apostles and elders** about this question* (Acts 15:2).

It is interesting that after they shared their testimonies with the church, they then met with the leaders of the New Testament church—the apostles and the elders:

*The **apostles and elders** met to consider this question* (Acts 15:6).

It is clear that the apostles were not necessarily the original 12 (although some of them were probably involved), but they met with the "new" apostles and the elders of the church. James appears to be the one who gave oversight to the apostles and elders in Jerusalem. He seemed to be the apostle who was responsible for the decision-making process. The next step was to send out men from their company to the Church throughout the known world, exhort them, and teach them:

When they finished, James spoke up: "Brothers, listen to me" (Acts 15:13).

*Then the **apostles and elders,** with the whole church, decided to choose some of their own men and send them to Antioch with Paul and Barnabas. They chose Judas (called Barsabbas) and Silas, two men who were leaders among the brothers* (Acts 15:22).

*As they traveled from town to town, they delivered the decisions reached by the **apostles and elders** in Jerusalem for the people to obey* (Acts 16:4).

Regardless of the terminology that today's church uses for leadership, there is a need for local leaders (elders) and leaders who have a larger sphere of spiritual responsibility (apostolic overseers). Paul the Apostle wrote to Titus and exhorted him to appoint elders in every city on the island of Crete.

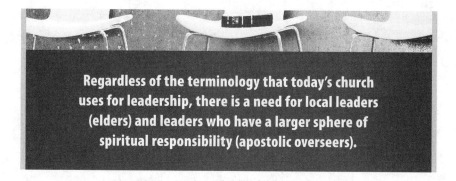

Regardless of the terminology that today's church uses for leadership, there is a need for local leaders (elders) and leaders who have a larger sphere of spiritual responsibility (apostolic overseers).

The reason I [Titus] left you in Crete was that you might straighten out what was left unfinished and appoint elders in every town, as I directed you (Titus 1:5).

In order to see the Church built from house to house in the nations of the world, we have come to believe that we must allow the Lord to raise up among us those with an apostolic-type ministry (those who oversee larger areas) and elders who serve in every city (local area).

Apostles

According to the New Testament, apostles are "foundation layers." These apostles also seemed to be gifted to give spiritual counsel, admonition, and oversight to local leadership teams. Many of Paul's letters serve as an example of the apostolic ministry that the Lord had given to him.

> *By the grace God has given me, I laid a foundation as an expert builder, and someone else is building on it. But each one should be careful how he builds. For no one can lay any foundation other than the one already laid, which is Jesus Christ* (1 Corinthians 3:10-11).

Bill Scheidler, in his book *The New Testament Church and Its Ministries*, gives the following insights on apostles:

The word "apostle" (Greek—*apostolos*) literally means "one who is sent forth." The word "apostle" was often used in the classical Greek world. It was used to refer to an emissary or ambassador; to a fleet of ships or an expedition sent forth with a specific objective; to the admiral who commanded the fleet or the colony which was founded by the admiral. If a fleet of ships left Rome with the purpose of establishing a new colony somewhere, all of these were called apostles—the fleet, the admiral, the new found colony.

The particular truth that is emphasized by this usage is the relationship of those who were sent to the sender. All of these, the admiral, the fleet, and the colony that was formed, represented a true image of the one by whom they were sent. In other words, they were faithful to transmit or reflect the intentions of the sender (Hebrews 3:1).

The primary attitude of a true apostle, then, must be faithfulness.[1]

An apostle, then, is one who is sent forth with authority, who faithfully represents the purposes and the intentions of the sender. There are at least 23 different apostles mentioned in the New Testament. There are also various types or classes of apostles and apostolic ministry mentioned in the Bible. For example:

1. Jesus Christ was and is the chief apostle.

Therefore, holy brothers, who share in the heavenly calling, fix your thoughts on Jesus, the apostle and high priest whom we confess (Hebrews 3:1).

2. The 12 apostles of the Lamb
The original 12 apostles are unique. No modern-day apostle can ever take the place of the original 12. (See Luke 6:12.)

The wall of the city had twelve foundations, and on them were the names of the twelve apostles of the Lamb (Revelation 21:14).

3. The James-type apostle
James gave oversight to the apostles and elders in Jerusalem. He seems to have basically stayed in one location.

When they finished, James spoke up: "Brothers, listen to me" (Acts 15:13).

The next day Paul and the rest of us went to see James, and all the elders were present (Acts 21:18).

4. The Paul-type apostle

Paul was a traveling apostle who had been given authority and responsibility by the Lord for churches in various parts of the world.

Paul, an apostle of Christ Jesus by the will of God, to the saints in Ephesus, the faithful in Christ Jesus (Ephesians 1:1).

It appears as if Paul was not necessarily recognized by every church as an apostle. He was, however, recognized by the churches that the Lord gave him spiritual responsibility for. He told the Corinthian Christians that his sphere of authority and responsibility included them.

We, however, will not boast beyond proper limits, but will confine our boasting to the field God has assigned to us, a field that reaches even to you (2 Corinthians 10:13).

5. The Timothy-type apostle

Timothy was sent by Paul for apostolic ministry to the Corinthian church. Although Paul was the "senior" apostle, the Corinthians also saw Timothy as having an apostolic ministry that would be used of the Lord to give them direction and guidance.

For this reason I am sending to you Timothy, my son whom I love, who is faithful in the Lord. He will remind you of my way of life in Christ Jesus, which agrees with what I teach everywhere in every church (1 Corinthians 4:17).

Paul sent other men who served on a team with him to fulfill an apostolic role in certain situations, just as he sent Timothy to Corinth. As I mentioned earlier, Paul sent Titus to Crete. Epaphras was used of the Lord to start the church in Colossae. To our knowledge, Paul never had the opportunity to go to the Colossian church personally. Nevertheless, he was still given apostolic authority from the Lord for this work. Epaphras also worked with Paul to oversee this work.

> *Epaphras, who is one of you and a servant of Christ Jesus, sends greetings. He is always wrestling in prayer for you, that you may stand firm in all the will of God, mature and fully assured* (Colossians 4:12).

6. *Those involved in apostolic-type ministry*

The 70 who were sent out were involved in apostolic-type ministry. Those within a small group or house church who have a God-given ability to plan ahead strategically for new groups to be birthed in your city may have a "seed" of apostolic ministry developing in their lives.

I grew up with the ability to play the guitar, but it was not until I was 16 years old that I actually started to practice and learn how to play. There are many future apostles in our midst today. They are presently being trained and groomed by the Holy Spirit to fulfill key roles in the Kingdom of God in the future. An apostolic call is not something we do because we think it sounds exciting. This gift is received from the Lord, and He will develop it. We believe the Lord will raise up modern-day apostles to train and develop future apostles.

> *Greet Andronicus and Junias, my relatives who have been in prison with me. They are outstanding among the apostles, and they were in Christ before I was* (Romans 16:7).

Our current understanding is that the Lord will call many apostolic-type overseers from the Church that He is building in this generation to serve His people. Some will serve the church in the local area and help to oversee dozens of congregations and house church networks and hundreds of small groups and house churches. Others will go to the nations of the world to help establish and oversee new works. Some will do both.

True apostolic overseers will have a father's heart for those whom the Lord has placed within their sphere of spiritual responsibility. Paul told the church of the Thessalonians:

> *You know we never used flattery, nor did we put on a mask to cover up greed—God is our witness. We were not looking for praise from men, not from you or anyone else.*
>
> *As apostles of Christ we could have been a burden to you, but we were gentle among you, like a mother caring for her little children. We loved you so much that we were delighted to share with you not only the gospel of God but our lives as well, because you had become so dear to us* (1 Thessalonians 2:5-8).

The person with a true apostolic ministry will respond to those within his care in the same way that a father will respond to his married children. He has authority because he is a spiritual father. However, he is careful to use that authority in a way that will undergird the local elders and the local church.

Some persons may be involved in more than one role at the same time. James and Peter seemed to be both apostles and elders (see 1 Pet. 5:1).

Elders

When believers are sick, they are instructed by the Scriptures to call for the elders of the church. James seems to be referring to the local elders.

> *Is any one of you sick? He should call the elders of the church to pray over him and anoint him with oil in the name of the Lord* (James 5:14).

Paul gives clear qualifications for the appointment of elders in First Timothy 3:1-7 and Titus 1:5-9:

The reason I left you in Crete was that you might straighten out what was left unfinished and appoint elders in every town, as I directed you. An elder must be blameless, the husband of but one wife, a man whose children believe and are not open to the charge of being wild and disobedient. Since an overseer is entrusted with God's work, he must be blameless—not overbearing, not quick-tempered, not given to drunkenness, not violent, not pursuing dishonest gain. Rather he must be hospitable, one who loves what is good, who is self-controlled, upright, holy and disciplined. He must hold firmly to the trustworthy message as it has been taught, so that he can encourage others by sound doctrine and refute those who oppose it (Titus 1:5-9).

In the New Testament, we see elders being appointed by those who give them apostolic oversight. Paul instructed Titus to appoint elders in Crete. We are told in the Book of Acts that Paul and Barnabas ordained elders in every church. The qualifications for elders are mostly character qualifications, not abilities. The only ability that is mentioned in the two lists mentioned in Scripture is the ability to teach.

Paul and Barnabas appointed elders for them in each church and, with prayer and fasting, committed them to the Lord, in whom they had put their trust (Acts 14:23).

Serving as an elder in the local church is both a privilege as well as a serious responsibility. Kevin Conner, in his book *The Church in the New Testament,* says:

If any man desire, "reach out after, long for, to covet, to stretch oneself" the office of a bishop, he should seek to qualify. It speaks of a deep inward drive or impulse to equip oneself for the ministry of an elder. It is a "good work" (1 Timothy 3:1). An excellent task. It is not a desire for a title or office position, but work! Matthew 23:1-12; Job 32:21-22. Not flattering titles. The office is work! As long as one is functioning in the office and working he is such. It is not holding titular power, or power of a title.[2]

It is our understanding that local elders serve and oversee God's people meeting in a given area. A primary responsibility is to serve and equip the small group leaders and house church leaders. They are also responsible before the Lord for equipping and encouraging of believers locally.

New Testament Elders Are Often Called "Pastors" Today

The senior leader of a local church or house church network, along with his leadership team, must have a pastor's heart for the people in the congregation. However, the primary gift the Lord places within him may not be that of a pastor. He could have a leadership gift, or an apostolic gift, or maybe a combination of various gifts. We think that the term "senior elder" and a "team of elders" may be more accurate to describe the leader of a congregation or house church network and his leadership team.

Nevertheless, you probably noticed that we used the term "senior elder" and "local pastor" interchangeably. Despite the fact that, for simplicity, we often call the senior elder of our congregations a "pastor," we realize that he may not have a pastoral anointing. If a senior elder does not have the gift of a pastor, the key is to have another person with a pastoral anointing as a vital part of that leader's team so the people will be cared for pastorally.

The role of the senior elder or local "pastor" in a cell-based church is to equip believers to do the work of ministry in small groups. House church network overseers train leaders to make disciples and lead house churches. This is quite different from our traditional thinking about the leader of a local church. The image of the pastor in today's church is that of a jack-of-all-trades: he is supposed to be a professional who can preach, visit the sick, balance the church budget, and offer every other type of spiritual service one can think of. In contrast, the focus of local church leadership in the New Testament was on training believers for the work of ministry and overseeing that work so the believers could minister effectively in small groups and house churches.

Simon and Andrew were fishermen who used nets to catch fish:

> *Then Jesus said to them, "Follow Me, and I will make you become fishers of men"* (Mark 1:17).

One of the "nets" the Lord has given us as we fish for men is small groups and house churches. Since all nets get worn and torn, they must be mended so the fish will not be lost through the holes. Who mends the nets? We believe the majority of net-mending is done by the leadership teams (elders and/or pastors) as they serve local congregations and house church networks.

The responsibility of the local pastor or house church network leader is not to sit behind a desk. His job is to spend time with the people. He builds (mends) relationships by praying, working, and spending time together with the people he serves. Local pastors go from home to home praying with small group leaders and house church leaders and helping them to hear from God a strategy for their small groups and house churches. This helps to ensure that there are no holes in the "net," so that no fish are lost, and so that new "fish" can be caught.

The elders also have the task of releasing the fivefold ministry (apostles, prophets, evangelists, pastors, and teachers) to equip and encourage the believers within the congregations and house church networks where they serve. Many times, elders also function in the fivefold ministry. We'll be talking more about this in the next chapter, and you can read more about the role of elders in a book I co-wrote with three friends in leadership, entitled *The Biblical Role of Elders in Today's Church.*[3]

God-appointed leadership

We see in the Scriptures that God appoints leadership over various spheres in His Kingdom. God uses these leaders to make decisions that affect those whom they serve. These leaders are called by the Lord to lead through servanthood. For example, husbands and wives are appointed by the Lord to give leadership to their families. God speaks to the family through the father and mother who serve in leadership in the home. The husband is appointed by God as the head of his household, yet he leads as a team with his wife. He is called to lay down his life for his wife and children. A wise father and mother will listen to their children before making decisions that will affect them.

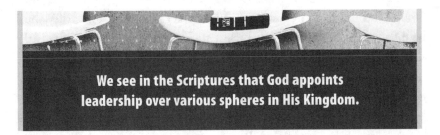

We see in the Scriptures that God appoints leadership over various spheres in His Kingdom.

In the church, God is raising up teams of elders and teams of apostolic leaders who will pray and work together. As these teams walk together in unity and listen to the wisdom of God that comes from those whom they serve, there should be clear headship among each team. There is headship in every realm and sphere of God's Kingdom. This person serves as the "primary vision carrier" for the group he is leading.

Both the Old and New Testament give numerous examples of this leadership principle. The Scriptures tell us in Numbers 27:16 (NKJV), *"Let the Lord...set a man over the congregation."* Although Moses worked closely with a leadership team (Aaron and Miriam), he was clearly anointed by God to lead the children of Israel. In the New Testament in Acts 13:13, we read about Paul and his party who were involved in establishing churches. In Acts 15:13-22, when the apostles and elders gathered together to make a doctrinal decision in the early church, after a time of discussion, James made the judgment as to what the decision should be. The other apostles and elders and the church confirmed the decision. Leadership in both the Old and New Testament did not work alone but with a team of leaders who served with them. Paul and Barnabas appointed elders in every church (see Acts 14:23).

It is amazing what the Lord will do when a team of people are willing to pray together and work as a team in complete unity and yet recognize godly appointed leadership among them. We use the analogy of a head and shoulders and body regarding church leadership. Psalm 133 gives a clear understanding of how head and shoulders and body leadership and decision-making works.

> *How good and pleasant it is when brothers live together in unity! It is like precious oil poured on the head, running down on the beard, running down on Aaron's beard, down upon the collar of his robes. It is as if the dew of Hermon were falling on Mount Zion. For there the Lord bestows His blessing, even life forevermore* (Psalm 133:1-3).

The head of every team needs to be properly attached to the shoulders (the others on the team) through a God-ordained relationship of trust and affirmation. If the head moves too far from the shoulders (by not honoring the team) or if the head is forced down (by the team not honoring the head), the body experiences a pain in the neck. If the head is appropriately attached to the shoulders (through relationship, trust, servanthood, prayer, and proper communication), and the shoulders support and affirm the head, the oil of the Holy Spirit will run down from the head to the shoulders to the body. As these servant leaders dwell together in the unity of Christ, God will command a blessing, as indicated in Psalm 133.

Decision-Making

We believe that leadership teams should strive to get the mind of the

Lord together through prayer and consensus whenever possible. However, there may be times when a consensus cannot be reached.

Although we should always try to reach complete agreement on every decision, we should not be bound by the need for unanimity. We call this "avoiding the rule of the negative." That is, if five on the team agree and one disagrees, under unanimity, the negative would carry the decision. This is spiritually dangerous. The entire team must clearly recognize the primary leader of the team, and after prayer and discussion if the team cannot come to complete agreement, he makes the decision. James the apostle had the same role in Acts 15. It is important to say, however, that the team leader should have "recognized spiritual fathers" in his life for accountability and to avoid the potential of autocratic leadership.

These leadership principles apply to any sphere of church leadership—the corporate church, the local congregation, the house church network, or the small group and house church. A wise leader of a congregation or house church network will always desire to involve his whole leadership team in decision-making. As the senior elder, he is responsible to discern what the Lord is saying through the team serving with him. The senior leader will assume his God-given leadership role and discern whether a consensus has been reached. If a decision must be made and there is not a complete consensus, the senior leader, after considering the input from each team member, needs to make the decision. However, the senior elder has final authority, not absolute authority. If there is conflict or an impasse in decision-making, apostolic overseers of the family of churches should provide an outside court of appeal for the senior elder and his team.

Although the final decisions affecting the local church or house church network are usually made by the eldership team, we should not forget that the wisdom of God is often evident in God's people in the church or house church network. Church leaders are also encouraged to draw from this wisdom from the Body before making decisions.

Experience God's Blessing

We have come to believe that regardless of the terminology the church at large uses today for leadership, there are local leaders (elders) and leaders who have a larger sphere of spiritual responsibility (apostolic-type overseers). We are fully persuaded at this time that both are needed in order to effectively reach an entire area for Christ. We further believe when a new church begins, it is necessary to allow time for growth before these two levels of leadership are established. It is spiritually healthy, though, for the leaders of the new church or house church network to be receiving input and counsel from a person or persons who have an apostolic call on their lives.

In the next chapter, we will look at two dead traditions I call the "holy man myth" and the "holy building myth" that plagues much of the church today and can hinder Christ's work. These two myths must be exposed and destroyed in order for the church of the 21st century to experience the end-time harvest the Lord has promised.

QUESTIONS TO THINK ABOUT
From Chapter 15

1. What are the scriptural responsibilities of apostolic overseers and elders?

2. Give a few examples from the Bible of the different types of apostolic ministry.

3. How can decisions be made in a godly way according to a biblical pattern found in Acts 15?

CHAPTER 16

Two Myths—Holy Men and Holy Buildings

Although it may often be hard to admit, many times we base our theology more on our preconceived ideas and our past experiences than we think. Many Baptists grow up with a Baptist understanding of the Scriptures, and they are convinced that "their" brand of theology is correct. This also applies to the Methodists, the Lutherans, the Charismatics...including you and me! So then, we need to be sure that what we believe about the church is based on the Scriptures and not on our own traditional understanding of the way things have been done in the past.

The Berean Christians refused to take everything that Paul preached at face value. They went home and studied the Scriptures to be sure that the things that Paul was saying were really true.

> *Now the Bereans were of more noble character than the Thessalonians, for they received the message with great*

eagerness and examined the Scriptures every day to see if what Paul said was true (Acts 17:11).

Is it possible that certain traditions that we consider to be completely scriptural, in reality, are not based on the Bible at all? Could it be that the real reason we do these things is because our spiritual parents and grandparents did them? We are creatures of habit who tend to gravitate toward our own traditions.

Did you ever hear of the young mother who always cut the ends off of the ham before baking it in the oven? When she was asked why she always followed this procedure, she said, "Because Grandma did it that way." Little did she know that Grandma's roast pan was too small for the entire ham; that was the only motivation Grandma had to cut off the ends! We need to know why we do what we do.

In the church, we constantly find ourselves following certain traditions. Some traditions are good; however, we need to be sure that our ways of thinking about the church are the same as God's. If they are not in accordance with the thoughts of God, we are probably following dead traditions. These traditions, then, are nothing more than myths. They must be replaced by the Word of God. Otherwise, the church will never be built from house to house, city to city, and nation to nation.

Let's look at two traditions that many Christians believe that hinder the work of the Lord in today's church. These myths must be replaced by the truth of God's Word. I call them "the holy man" and "the holy building" myths.

The Holy Man Myth

Many Christians today have set up the pastor of the local church as the "holy man." They have elevated the pastors and the priests as holy men who stand between them and the Lord. The Scriptures teach us otherwise. The Bible tells us that we are all kings and priests (see Rev. 1:6). We all have direct access to the Lord through the shed blood of Jesus Christ.

A pastor is literally a "shepherd." He cares for the "sheep." And this caring for the sheep has nothing to do with his position but with the gifts and calling that the Lord has placed on his life. He just loves people! A pastor is a people person.

In today's world, with the tradition of calling the leader of the local church a "pastor," the pastoral title has been elevated above the other ministry gifts in the fourth chapter of Ephesians. This can be detrimental to the growth of God's Kingdom. Here's why. The pastor becomes the "holy man," and he performs his services in a "holy building." Instead of each believer realizing that he is a vital part of the Lord's spiritual army, the believers begin to look to this "holy man" rather than the Lord. Then we give him a title—Pastor Bob or Pastor Jack.

First of all, a most important thing to consider is that the primary leader of the local church is called by the Lord and anointed for leadership. Does he have a leadership gift and a calling from the Lord to be the leader of the church he is leading? Imagine a band playing. Is the lead singer always the leader of the band? Or is the drummer the leader? Perhaps the guitarist leads. It depends—the real leader is that person who has the ability and the "call" to lead the band, regardless of his ability to play a certain instrument.

We believe the leader of a local church should have a shepherd's heart for God's people, even though the ministry gift in operation in his life may not be that of a pastor. If he does not have the gift of a pastor, it's important that he has an individual serving alongside him with a pastoral gift to look after the needs of the people.

Of course, if the primary leader of the church truly has the gift of a pastor, we are not saying it is wrong to call him the pastor. We just believe that it may not always be the best terminology to use. The term "senior elder" or "lead elder" may be a more scriptural term to use according to our understanding of the Bible.

To the elders among you, I appeal as a fellow elder, a witness
of Christ's sufferings and one who also will share in the glory

to be revealed: Be shepherds of God's flock that is under your care, serving as overseers—not because you must, but because you are willing, as God wants you to be; not greedy for money, but eager to serve; not lording it over those entrusted to you, but being examples to the flock (1 Peter 5:1-3).

All Believers Are Called to Minister

The holy man myth tells us that the pastor is responsible for the entire ministry in the church. The truth is that all believers are called to be equipped to be ministers.

It was He who gave some to be apostles, some to be prophets, some to be evangelists, and some to be pastors and teachers, to prepare God's people for works of service, so that the body of Christ may be built up (Ephesians 4:11-12).

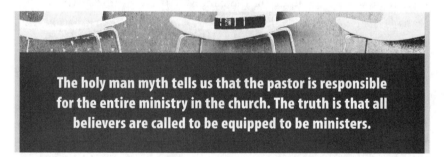

The holy man myth tells us that the pastor is responsible for the entire ministry in the church. The truth is that all believers are called to be equipped to be ministers.

Our view is that this holy man myth must be replaced by the Word of God in order for the church to be effective today. The pastor's responsibility must be to equip believers to minister! Thousands of pastors are burning out today because they are missing this truth. They spend the bulk of their time ministering instead of training the believers to minister. Without building on an underground pattern, it is almost impossible not to burn out! Remember, Jesus said that His yoke is easy and His burden is light. But it must be His burden!

For example, if there is a need for counseling, rather than automatically expecting the pastor to have all the answers, believers should allow the pastor or another qualified individual to train them to counsel and exhort others. The next time they can be the ones the Lord uses to set people free.

Another way this myth surfaces in the traditional church is that the "pastor" is expected to preach every Sunday. We believe the Lord's best is for the church to be built as apostles, prophets, evangelists, pastors, and teachers encourage and equip believers from house to house and from congregation to congregation. If any of these gifts are not yet developed in your local church or house church network, bring in the fivefold ministers and their ministry gifts from other parts of the Body of Christ. These proven ministers will help to identify and cultivate the gifts from within your local church or house church network.

Proven Ministers—The "Fivefold Ministry"

There are five gifts mentioned in Ephesians 4:11-12, often called the fivefold ministry gifts. Our understanding is that the fivefold ministry gifts are equipping gifts given to us by Jesus Himself to train and encourage the Body of Christ. They are not necessarily synonymous with governmental leadership positions, like elders. Many times these fivefold ministers will serve in areas of church government; however, it is not primarily because of the ministry gift that they have but because the Lord has called them to this area of governmental leadership.

Our view is that many of these "fivefold" ministry gifts are for trans-local ministry, not to be used solely in one small group, house church, or congregation, as seen in Acts 15:22,30-32,35. We have come to believe that these gifts should be used from house to house and from congregation to congregation as much as possible. Sometimes the pastor, who has a shepherd's heart for the people in a given area, may not travel as much as the other fivefold ministers. On the other hand, some pastors may serve as "pastors to pastors" and subsequently be more involved in traveling ministry.

We have also discovered that most people with fivefold ministry gifts have a "gift mix." For example, someone may be a prophetic teacher or a teaching evangelist. It seems to us that the apostle, prophet, evangelist, pastor, and teacher must learn how to function together in order for the church of Jesus Christ to come to a place of maturity. Is it possible that much of what we have seen regarding the five gifts working together has been manufactured in the minds of man more than it has been the plan of God? We have been involved in various teams and have made sincere attempts to somehow cause these gifts to work together. We have simply not seen the fivefold ministry work properly yet. But we believe it is the will of God for the fivefold ministry to function together and to equip and encourage the church as the Body of Christ matures in the days ahead. We wait with great expectation what the Lord will reveal to us in the future.

From our limited understanding, here is one reason that we believe it has not worked yet. The gifts of apostle, prophet, evangelist, pastor, and teacher are anointed leadership gifts for the purpose of equipping, encouraging, and training the church, rather than governmental leadership positions in the Body of Christ. We may have a tendency to confuse these two types of leadership in the church—anointed equipping leadership and anointed governmental leadership.

Apostles are given to the church to help us receive a vision from the Lord to reach the world. Prophets are given to train us to listen to the voice of God. Evangelists are called of God to stir us and train us to reach pre-Christians. Pastors are commissioned by the Lord to encourage us and show us how to make disciples! And teachers have a divine anointing to assist us in understanding the Word of God. These ministry gifts should be ministering to every level of the church: to individuals, families, small groups, house churches, congregations, movements, and the church at large.

Will some of these fivefold ministry gifts be involved in leadership as an overseer or an elder? Of course they will. We just cannot try to program it! We are of the persuasion that the church that is going to grow is the church that makes sure they are receiving a regular impartation from each of these ministry gifts while realizing that only Jesus has all of the gifts.

This is the reason it is important for people with the various gifts to minister the Word at the small group, the house church, the congregational gatherings, and large corporate meetings. We need to hear from each of the five ministry gifts. If your small group or house church is lacking a zeal for evangelism, ask an evangelist to come to your meetings and minister to you for a few weeks. Then see if any of the believers in your group are willing to go with him to explain his faith with a person who has not yet made a decision to follow Christ. You will be amazed at the results!

Although we confirm the need to sit under the public preaching of the Word, preaching and teaching are not the only ways we can receive an impartation from these gifts. For example, the best way to receive an impartation from a pastor may be to join him while he imparts the truth of the Word of God to someone who is in a crisis. Perhaps the church has been too narrow-minded about the way we can be equipped by the fivefold ministry.

For more on how the fivefold ministry was created to work within the local church and house churches, read Ron Myer's book, *Fivefold Ministry Made Practical.*[1]

Deacons Are Ministers

Some believers teach that deacons are no longer needed in today's church. In other Christian circles, people believe that deacons function as the leadership board of the local church. We are fully convinced that literally thousands of deacons need to be released to prepare for the coming revival. These deacons are not a church governmental board but instead a group of servants who are released to obey the living God. The word *deacon* literally means "a servant" or "a minister."

> *In those days when the number of disciples was increasing, the Grecian Jews among them complained against the*

Hebraic Jews because their widows were being overlooked in the daily distribution of food. So the Twelve gathered all the disciples together and said, "It would not be right for us to neglect the ministry of the word of God in order to wait on tables. Brothers, choose seven men from among you who are known to be full of the Spirit and wisdom. We will turn this responsibility over to them and will give our attention to prayer and the ministry of the word." This proposal pleased the whole group. They chose Stephen, a man full of faith and of the Holy Spirit; also Philip, Procorus, Nicanor, Timon, Parmenas, and Nicolas from Antioch, a convert to Judaism. They presented these men to the apostles, who prayed and laid their hands on them. So the word of God spread. The number of disciples in Jerusalem increased rapidly, and a large number of priests became obedient to the faith (Acts 6:1-7).

Deacons, likewise, are to be men worthy of respect, sincere, not indulging in much wine, and not pursuing dishonest gain (1 Timothy 3:8).

Deacons serve in hands-on ministry in the church. Again, we have come to believe that the closest scriptural example that we have of a small group leader is the ministry of the deacon. We are not saying that small group leaders should be called deacons; however, we do believe there is a resemblance between New Testament deacons and small group leaders. Although there may be many types of deacons, the small group leader seems to function in many ways as a New Testament deacon, in that he is called to practical spiritual service.

The Holy Building Myth

The Church is people, or literally, "called-out ones." The buildings and meetings that are used must serve the people and the purposes of God. The people cannot be serving the building or the meeting.

We sometimes call this the "holy building" myth. Somehow the Church today has been led to believe that the church building is a holy place. Nearly everything spiritual is supposed to center around the holy building. In reality, it is we who are believers in Jesus Christ who are holy, not a church building.

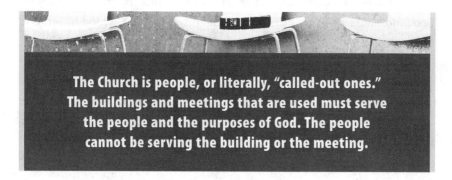

The Church is people, or literally, "called-out ones." The buildings and meetings that are used must serve the people and the purposes of God. The people cannot be serving the building or the meeting.

I was talking to a pastor on the staff of a large mega-church one day, and he told me that there were so many meetings and programs in the church building that the people did not have time to really minister in the small groups that were being established from house to house. I asked this pastor, "Why don't you close down some of your midweek meetings in your building to give God's people more time to develop relationships and practical outreach in the small groups?"

I will never forget his response. "If we stop having some of our public meetings, our offerings will go down. And if our offerings go down, the large building that we are meeting in will be used as an airplane hanger instead of a church facility." The mortgage on the building had to be paid. They were slaves to their building.

What is the first thing that you think of when someone uses the word "church"? Most of us think of a building that has been dedicated to the Lord for His people to meet in. But that is not a church. The Church is people!

During one of my first trips to Scotland, I was introduced to a new term, "haggis." When I inquired about this new word, my Scottish friends decided to play a trick on me. They told me that a haggis was an animal that lived on the hills. Due to the hills being so steep, they felt that it was important for me to know that the haggis's legs were longer on one side than on the other so that they could walk on the side of mountains without falling over. Ridiculous! And yet, when I thought of the word "haggis," I would visualize this peculiar animal roaming the hills of Scotland. Later I was told the truth. Haggis was actually a food to eat, not a rare, lopsided Scottish animal!

Until we begin to visualize the Church as she really is—a group of people bought by the blood of Jesus Christ, who are in a relationship with Him and with one another with a vision to reach the world—we will continue to think in terms of buildings instead of people. It is like an army thinking that the real army is the barracks instead of the soldiers.

> *And I also say to you that you are Peter, and on this rock I will build My church, and the gates of Hades shall not prevail against it* (Matthew 16:18).

Jesus was not thinking about bricks and mortar when He said that He would build His Church. He was thinking about His people whom He would empower with the Holy Spirit and send from house to house into every strata of society for the furtherance of His Kingdom. Let's make a decision today to change our way of thinking. Instead of emphasizing "going to church," let's be the Church.

Let's dream together in the next chapter about the Church truly being the Church that Jesus Christ intends to come back for.

QUESTIONS TO THINK ABOUT
From Chapter 16

1. How can we "honor" our leaders without making them into "holy men"?

2. What is the responsibility of every believer?

3. What effect do the fivefold ministry gifts have on the church? How can these ministry gifts help a small group or house church or congregation?

4. How is a small group leader similar to a deacon?

CHAPTER 17

Let's Dream Together

Rev. Martin Luther King, Jr., slain civil rights leader in America, had a dream to see racial equality become a reality. I too, have a dream. I have a dream...to see the Church become a reflection of the image of Christ. I dream that the Church will be the grassroots movement we have been called to be, as we serve the Lord from house to house, city to city, and nation to nation.

It Happened in a Home

I love to read the Book of Acts. It seems like everywhere the apostles went, there was either a revival or a riot. Paul and Silas went to Philippi and cast a demon out of a fortune teller. Her masters were irate and threw Paul and Silas into prison. So they started singing hymns and the Lord sent an earthquake. The jailer was so shook up he was going to take his life, but Paul quickly assured him that the prisoners were all still there in the prison. Let's pick up on the story.

He then brought them out and asked, "Sirs, what must I do to be saved?"

> They replied, "Believe in the Lord Jesus, and you will be saved—you and your **household**." Then they spoke the word of the Lord to him and to all the others in his **house**. At that hour of the night the jailer took them and washed their wounds; then immediately he and all his family were baptized. The jailer brought them into his **house** and set a meal before them; he was filled with joy because he had come to believe in God—he and his whole family (Acts 16:30-34).

These guys were amazing! Paul and Silas had just experienced imprisonment, a beating, and an earthquake. Yet they were prepared to experience a move of God, in the home of the jailer. It was quite an unconventional place for a revival.

Rick Joyner, in his book *The Harvest,* believes that in the next revival in the Church, one of the greatest tools that the Lord will use for equipping His people will be "home groups."

> Literally hundreds of thousands of couples will begin to open their homes to small groups. These couples will be equipped to lead the lost to Christ, cast out demons, heal the sick and lay a strong biblical foundation in the lives of new believers. These will not become isolated home churches but will be used to incorporate multitudes of new believers into larger congregations. After they have brought a group of new believers to a place of stability and function in the church they will begin with another group of new believers.

Ultimately, home groups will become the foundation upon which the entire church is being built. Home group ministry teams will actually provide the bulk of the work in equipping the saints, including teaching and pastoring. Without these small ministry teams church leaders would be quickly overwhelmed by the massive task of the harvest.[1]

We agree. We believe the next revival will happen in all sorts of unconventional places, including homes, offices, parks, coffee shops, and warehouses.

Mega-churches and Community Churches

We cannot place God in a box, however. He will move regardless of our structures. We firmly believe He will move within the different types of churches we have today. Let's take a look at the type of church structures around us. First there are the mega-churches. They usually use one building that becomes the center for "ministry." In a mega-church you will often find a clear vision and a real sense of unity as the Lord's people work together with a common purpose. Many times a gifted charismatic leader is found at the helm of this type of church. The Lord has used mega-churches during the past 25 years in a marvelous way; however, some mega-churches may have some deficiencies.

Karen Hurston, who has spent many years of her life studying churches, told me once that many mega-churches are more like teaching centers. This is a bold analysis, but in some cases she may be right. One of the difficulties that many mega-churches have is that many believers are bench warmers and never use the many gifts that the Lord has given to them because they get "lost in the crowd."

Another type of church that we can find in our communities is the community church. One church outgrows its building, and a group is sent out to start another congregation. Praise God for many, many wonderful community churches today. There are also many new churches that are linked together by an "apostolic fellowship" or some type of denomination. The positive trait that you can find in many denominations is the freedom for each new congregation to use the gifts that it has. Many people get involved in the work of the Kingdom. Some denominations have a focus on their central denominational headquarters, while others continue to grow with little "control from the top."

One of the difficulties that some denominations have is a constant struggle between the vision of a "central headquarters" versus the vision of a local church(es). When a lack of unity comes into a denominational structure, they usually lose their spiritual momentum and fervency for prayer. Believers are no longer focused on Jesus and the harvest, because they are too focused on each other. The result sometimes is spiritual barrenness.

A Grassroots Movement

This brings us to a type of church that is growing exponentially throughout many nations—the grassroots movement. This type of church is being modeled for us in various parts of the world today. I mentioned the church in Ethiopia, which is modeling this type of church. The church in China is also an example. The church in the Book of Acts was a grassroots movement of the Holy Spirit as was the Methodist revival in the 18th century.

All grassroots church movements seem to have some common denominators. First of all, they usually meet in small groups for mutual accountability and discipleship. Second, nearly every member is involved in the work of ministry—a participant and not a bystander. Third, those in leadership are often average, common people who know that they have a big God living inside of them.

When they saw the courage of Peter and John and realized that they were unschooled, ordinary men, they were astonished and they took note that these men had been with Jesus (Acts 4:13).

A fourth common denominator in grassroots church movements seems to be an emphasis on prayer. The Moravians prayed in agreement around the clock for 100 years!

And a fifth common denominator appears to be the use of roving preachers/teachers who went from town to town and from house to house. These "circuit riders" kept the revival fire alive.

Today there are movements of the Holy Spirit that are following these five common denominators. I personally believe para-church ministries like YWAM and Campus Crusade for Christ are grassroots movements. They emphasize having a common vision and exhort their constituency to maintain a close relationship with Jesus and have a vision to reach the world and make disciples.

Sometimes we get so caught up in church programs and committees that we miss it. It is not too late! We believe that one of the reasons the Lord has raised up para-church ministries is to be examples of grassroots movements to our generation.

Part of the secret to grassroots movements is that clusters of believers work together with a common purpose. Yet there is a tremendous amount of flexibility for each group of believers to continue to expand and work together with other groups to build the Kingdom of God. Some church growth consultants today call this type of church a meta-church. Carl George, in his book *Prepare Your Church for the Future,* says:

> The prefix meta- means "change," as in *meta*bolism, *meta*-morphosis, *meta*physical, and the Greek word *metanoia* ("to change one's mind" or "repent").[2]

We have come to believe that a true meta-church then is a grassroots movement that is constantly willing to change the structure in order to obey the Holy Spirit's direction to prepare laborers for the coming harvest.

For example, the bones of a physical body provide the structure that is needed to remain healthy as a human being. As we grow, our bones must continue to grow properly to facilitate the rest of our body functions. The same principle applies to the Church of Jesus Christ. Our church structures must be constantly changing in order to serve the Kingdom of God growing in our midst; however, structure is necessary. Without a bone structure, our body would be a pile of nerves, arteries, muscles, and skin lying on the floor. Without an appropriate Church structure, the Church of Jesus Christ cannot function properly. But the focus is not on the structure; our focus must be on Jesus Christ and on people.

The Book of Acts is an excellent example of a grassroots (or ground swell) movement as the Holy Spirit moved from house to house, city to city, and nation to nation. When the apostles and elders met in Jerusalem to make decisions on certain issues that were affecting the church, the church leaders sent the prophets and teachers back to the churches to give their verdict, teaching the Word of God and encouraging the believers (see Acts 15 and 16) with the result that the church continued to grow.

Some of the dangers that face grassroots movements are exclusiveness, heresy, and pride. These dangers can be eliminated if the spiritual leaders are accountable and open with leaders in other parts of the Body of Christ. We need each other.

No matter what the structure, we believe the key is that the structure that is created must allow for the free expression of the creative abilities of God's people within that structure. The most efficient and effective structures are those where the individual can be seen and utilized, rather than disenfranchised or ignored.

In his book *The Church at the End of the Twentieth Century*, Francis Schaeffer described the necessity of understanding that God has created the form with which we have to live within—but He allows considerable freedom within that form. Francis and Edith Schaeffer opened their home in Switzerland to be a place where people might find satisfying answers to their questions and practical demonstration of Christian community. It was called L'Abri, the French word for "shelter," because they sought to provide a shelter from the pressures of a relentlessly secular society. Schaeffer understood that in a loving environment where community was practiced, people could find a voice and find their way, thus allowing God to use each one in the work of ministry.

Impacting the Marketplace

Everyone has a calling from God as an individual. Being called into church leadership is not more important, from God's perspective, than a calling into marketplace ministry. Some Christians feel apologetic about their role in the marketplace, but they do not have to. Christian believers must take the Word of God literally and begin to apply it where they spend 60 to 70 percent of their waking hours—at their workplaces. They can use their spiritual authority in their work lives, reflecting their spiritual value system in their area of influence. And small groups and house churches found in places of business are dynamic. Let's take the church to the people!

In order for us to effectively experience the Kingdom of God in every area of society and true transformation in our cities and regions, we must disciple both the present and the next generation to focus on their God-given call to "seven mountains of influence" that shape society. These seven mountains include the family, the church, business, government, education, the arts, and media. New unconventional churches will spring up in the future with a clear focus on each of these areas of influence, and we need to be ready to embrace God's people as they start these new churches, new wineskins, so to speak, that will look much different than what we have been familiar with. Many of these new churches will be micro-churches that will focus on one or more of these mountains of influence that will bring societal transformation.

Preparing for the Future

Now is the time to prepare for the future. I dream about the Church of Jesus Christ experiencing a new flexibility in the coming days. We are starting to see it. New house churches are being birthed by the Holy Spirit to provide new wineskins for the coming harvest. They network with the Church that Jesus is building throughout the world. In some cases, homes are being used for these churches to meet in and the money that is saved on building rental and maintenance is given to the poor and to missions and to the support of the fivefold ministry gifts that the Lord has given to equip the Body of Christ.

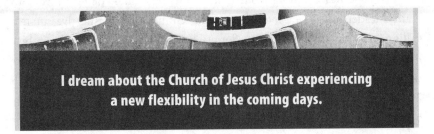

I dream about the Church of Jesus Christ experiencing a new flexibility in the coming days.

Small groups and house churches could meet in smaller homes, and larger homes could be used for celebration meetings for everyone involved. Every few months a large auditorium or amphitheater could be rented for a massive celebration of believers involved in small groups and house churches throughout the area. All of the churches in a given area could begin to share their resources and support, various gifts of administrations, counseling and apostolic ministry for sending missionaries, and so forth.

A team of apostolic overseers would give oversight to the Church in a given area; however, they would not be involved in the majority of the decision-making. They would only concern themselves with the basic values and guiding principles of the Christian revival movement. Local elders would handle the majority of the decision-making at the local level. People would be added to the Church daily as they come to faith in Christ. And everyone would be involved in making disciples. As someone said recently, "When revival hits, everyone will need to be a small group leader." And true spiritual fathers and mothers will serve as servant leaders for these small groups and house churches.

As we look to the future, we can expect the Lord to teach all of us to be flexible as we receive direction from Him. New types of small groups, house churches, and congregations will spring up to take care of the harvest. I was speaking at a seminar and met a woman who told me she leads a small group meeting at midnight. She ministers to people who work the second shift. That's flexibility!

Some congregations will meet in homes or house churches, releasing more money for missions rather than putting it into rent, mortgages, or maintenance. Other congregations will be led of the Lord to purchase, rent, or build facilities for teaching and training and to provide a place for outreach for those who have not yet determined to follow Christ in their communities.

Apostles, prophets, evangelists, pastors, and teachers will go from house to house and from congregation to congregation to train and encourage believers to minister in the love and power of our Lord Jesus Christ. Pastors will also equip believers in Christ to make disciples in each local area.

Local elders will serve God's people in their local congregations and house church networks. Apostolic overseers will be free to spend time in prayer, in ministering the Word, and continuing to give clear direction for the whole church under the anointing of the Holy Spirit. These apostolic-type overseers will lead more by influence than by hands-on management. They would be more concerned about undergirding believers through prayer and encouragement rather than in "leading from the top."

Teams of prophets will relate to the apostolic overseers on a regular basis as they receive messages from the Lord. The apostolic gifts need the prophetic gifts to stay on track. Dick Iverson from Portland, Oregon, points out that "the apostle is objective in nature, while the prophet is subjective in nature." And Kevin Conner from Melbourne, Australia, confirms this by adding, "Apostles and prophets are especially called to work together, each balancing the other."[3]

Some small group leaders and house church leaders will serve in a deacon-type role while others will serve in a pastoral role, serving the people of God and making disciples from house to house. They model New Testament hospitality. The home will be the main center for ministry.

We can expect to experience real joy as we work together as the church in each community. At certain times, hundreds of churches in a given area will close down their Sunday morning services and meet together as a sign to the world that the Body of Christ is one as the Father and the Son are one. In some parts of the country, sports stadiums could be utilized for these massive celebration meetings.

As we meet weekly in local congregations, small groups and house churches, our communities will be reached for Christ. Apostles and missionaries will continue to be sent out to the nations as churches are planted throughout the world. The young and the old will labor together as the Lord turns the hearts of the fathers to the children and the hearts of the children to their fathers (see Mal. 4:6).

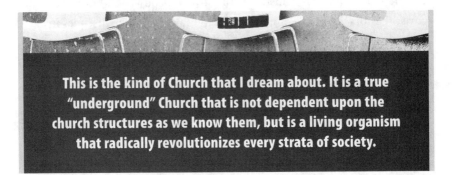

This is the kind of Church that I dream about. It is a true "underground" Church that is not dependent upon the church structures as we know them, but is a living organism that radically revolutionizes every strata of society.

The Church will work together internationally as the Lord sovereignly ordains international networks of apostolic leaders. These leaders will submit to one another and build the Church on the continents of the world. Modern-day prophets will be assisting them in this work. There is no competition in the Kingdom of God, and the Church will experience a laboring together that will make the world systems around us sit up and take notice. There are various anointings and spiritual insights that believers from different nations and continents have that we all need. There is no group of believers in any one city, nation, or continent that has it all.

The Lord has made His Body in a way that we all need to be dependent upon one another.

This is the kind of Church that I dream about and expect to experience in the coming days. It is a true "underground" Church that is not dependent upon the church structures as we know them, but is a living organism that radically revolutionizes every strata of society. Believers meeting together from house to house with a vision burning in their hearts for the cities and the nations of the world will give honor and glory to Jesus Christ, the Lord of all Lords and the King of all Kings.

QUESTIONS TO THINK ABOUT
From Chapter 17

1. Do you believe the house-to-house concept is one of the Lord's strategies to evangelize the whole world? Explain.

2. Give five common characteristics of grassroots movements.

3. What would you do if all the church buildings were closed down by the government?

Practical Application in the DCFI Family

The DOVE Christian Fellowship International family of churches is committed to our Lord and to the small group "underground" principles found in this book. This is how we seek to apply these principles in our network of churches.

Redwood trees are known to be some of the largest trees in the world. The secret of their ability to stand tall is not in their deep root system. The secret is in the fact that the roots of the trees are interconnected with the roots of the trees growing around them. They are interdependent. Each one needs the others. Our family of churches is committed by relationship and a common vision to start new churches worldwide.

Our desire is to see churches planted in clusters in the same geographical area so spiritual leaders can easily meet together for prayer and mutual encouragement and find ways to be more effective in building His

Kingdom together. Like the redwoods, they become interdependent upon one another.

The Blessing of Teamwork

Senior elders of DOVE churches in Pennsylvania and the surrounding states have the blessing of meeting together regularly for prayer and mutual encouragement. An Apostolic Council member also is committed to meet at least once each month individually with each senior elder. We maintain contact monthly with all senior elders.

The Lord, by His grace, has given us an extraordinary support team at DCFI. This team consists of the International Apostolic Council, Regional Apostolic Councils established throughout the world serving local church leaders in six continents, fivefold translocal ministers, and various ministries like the Stewardship Team, which handles financial matters. All are committed to resource the leadership and believers in DCFI partner churches and serve the greater Body of Christ. These various ministries offer leadership training and ministry development on many levels. For example, Peter Bunton, Ron Myer, Ibrahim Omondi, Steve Prokopchak, Brian Sauder, and I currently serve on the DCFI International Apostolic Council, traveling regularly to churches throughout the nations as we train leaders.

As was mentioned earlier, a few years ago, we recognized the need to more effectively train cell-based and house church leaders and church planters. Recognizing this need resulted in starting the "Church Planting and Leadership School." This 135-session leadership training school is producing lasting fruit by giving practical, scriptural leadership tools for both present and future small group leaders, elders, and church planters.

Since many who wanted to receive this training could not move to Pennsylvania to participate in the school, we also produced a video correspondence school in three modules. This training is now being utilized by churches from different denominations and movements throughout the United States, Canada, and in six continents of the world.

Prayer Is the Key to the Harvest

An important 24-hour prayer ministry includes a team of "prayer generals" who recruit, train, and encourage a team of "prayer warriors" responsible to cover segments of time each week to pray for the entire DCFI family of churches. These "prayer generals" and "prayer warriors" are scattered throughout the nations of the world.

Resourcing the Body of Christ

What the Lord has given to us, He has called us to openly share with the rest of the Body of Christ. It will take all the existing churches and millions of new churches working together to see the harvest reaped. A team of experienced leaders from DCFI travel the world training church leaders throughout the Body of Christ in cell-based and house church ministry and practical Christian living through seminars and conferences at various times throughout the year to serve and resource the broader Body of Christ. Publications tools and resources from House to House Publications are used by churches of many denominations and movements throughout the United States, Canada, and the world.

The International Apostolic Council and leadership from DCFI partner churches worldwide meet together each March for an annual International Leadership Conference for the purpose of mutual encouragement, leadership training, relationship building, and to receive a common vision from the Lord. The Lord has called us to work as a team together—with a shared vision, shared values, a shared procedure, and to build together by relationship. In order for the DCFI family of churches and ministries to be effective in laboring together, our procedure is written in a publication called the *DCFI Leadership Handbook.*[1]

Empowering the Next Generation

Each generation is different and has different needs and preferences.

We are committed to empowering, releasing, and supporting the next generation as they fulfill their particular call in God.

As Elisha received a double portion of the spirit that was on Elijah, our desire is to see our spiritual children far exceed us in developing their spiritual gifts and church leadership. Believers will be called to various areas of leadership: small group and house church leadership, local church leadership, fivefold ministry, and apostolic leadership. Many spiritual leaders will be called to focus on the marketplace.

The long-term goal of DCFI is to continue to establish many more apostolic councils in various regions of the world. Ibrahim Omondi, from Nairobi, Kenya, gives oversight to an apostolic leadership team made up of African leaders who are responsible for oversight of DCFI churches in Africa. The leadership for the DCFI movement is an International Apostolic Council, whose members include apostolic leaders from various nations.

As an international family of churches and ministries, we are called to keep actively involved in what the Lord is doing in the world and participate in the present expressions of His anointing. We desire to empower, train, and release God's people at the grassroots level to fulfill His purposes. After all, it happened 2,000 years ago in the Book of Acts. Let's join together as the Body of Christ, and in obedience to our God, trust Him to experience the Book of Acts again!

APPENDIX B

DCFI's Vision, Mission, and Values

DCFI (DOVE Christian Fellowship International) is an international apostolic family of churches and ministries from six continents of the world. We share common vision, mission, values, goals, and a commitment to plant and nurture churches and ministries throughout the nations.

As DOVE Christian Fellowship International, we are called to build the Church from house to house, city to city, and nation to nation through small groups.

This apostolic movement has a God-given authority and responsibility to serve, train, equip, release, and protect the people, ministries, and churches throughout the movement and advance the Kingdom of God.

DOVE is an acronym that states, "Declaring Our Victory Emmanuel." We are called as an international family to declare our victory in Emmanuel (God with us).

For more about DCFI, visit www.dcfi.org

DOVE Christian Fellowship International
Vision, Mission, and Values

Our Vision

To build a relationship with Jesus, with one another, and to reach the world from house to house, city to city, nation to nation.

Our Mission—Prayer, Evangelism, and Discipleship

Our mission is to exalt Jesus Christ as Lord, obey His Word, and to encourage and equip each believer for the work of ministry. This mission will essentially be accomplished by the threefold mandate God has given us: prayer, evangelism, and discipleship.

Prayer

In prayer we worship God; we bring our needs and the needs of the world to Him; and we allow the Holy Spirit to transform us, to empower us, and to reveal to us His specific strategies for fulfilling the Great Commission.

Evangelism

Through evangelism we seek to make known the glory of God and the name of Christ through verbal proclamation, publishing, the arts, acts of compassion and service, both to our own neighbors and cities, and also by going to the peoples of the world in cross-cultural mission. We desire to see children, youth, and adults come to a saving knowledge of the Lord Jesus Christ, the un-evangelized hear the Good News, and churches planted in all nations.

Discipleship

Engaging in discipleship, we build relationships with and care for one another, training each other in godliness and good works, so that we would all be mature disciples engaged in the threefold mission of prayer, evangelism, and discipleship. Discipleship thus becomes ongoing, as those who have been trained in turn train and disciple others.

We engage in this mission in humility, with dependence on God, and in cooperation with all brothers and sisters in the Body of Christ, working for unity in all that we do.

Our Values

All values and guiding principles for the DOVE Christian Fellowship International family must be rooted in the Scriptures (see 2 Tim. 3:16-17; 2 Tim. 2:15). DOVE is an acronym: Declaring Our Victory Emmanuel (God with us).

1. *Knowing God the Father through His Son Jesus Christ and living by His Word is the foundation of life.*

We believe that the basis of the Christian faith is to know God through repentance for sin, receiving Jesus Christ as Lord, building an intimate relationship with Him, and being conformed into His image. God has declared us righteous through faith in Jesus Christ (see John 1:12; 17:3; Rom. 8:29; 2 Cor. 5:21).

2. *It is essential for every believer to be baptized with the Holy Spirit and be completely dependent on Him.*

We recognize that we desperately need the person and power of the Holy Spirit to minister effectively to our generation. Changed lives are not the product of men's wisdom, but in the demonstration of the power of the Holy Spirit as modeled in the New Testament church (see 1 Cor. 2:2-5; John 15:5). We believe it is essential for every believer to be baptized with the Holy Spirit and to pursue spiritual gifts (see 2 Cor. 13:14; John 4:23-24).

All decisions need to be made by listening to the Holy Spirit as we make prayer a priority and learn to be worshipers. Worship helps us focus on the Lord and allows us to more clearly hear His voice.

We recognize that we do not wrestle against flesh and blood, but against demonic forces. Jesus Christ is our Lord, our Savior, our Healer, and our Deliverer (see Eph. 6:12; 1 John 3:8).

3. The Great Commission will be completed through prayer, evangelism, discipleship, and church planting.

We are committed to helping fulfill the Great Commission through prayer and fasting, evangelism, discipleship, and church planting locally, nationally, and internationally, reaching both Jew and Gentile (see Matt. 6:5-18; 28:19-20; Acts 1:8).

We are called to support others who are called as co-laborers, as churches are planted throughout the world. The Great Commission is fulfilled through tearing down spiritual strongholds of darkness and church planting (see 1 Cor. 3:6-9; Matt. 11:12; 2 Cor. 10:3-4; Acts 14:21-23).

We are also called to proclaim the Gospel through the arts, publications, and the media and will continue to believe God to raise up other resources and ministries to assist us in building the Church (see 1 Cor. 9:19-22).

4. We deeply value the sacred covenant of marriage and the importance of training our children to know Christ.

It is our belief that marriage and family are instituted by God, and healthy, stable families are essential for the Church to be effective in fulfilling its mission. Parents are called by God to walk in the character of Christ and to train their children in the nurture and loving discipline of the Lord Christ (see Mark 10:6-8; Eph. 5:22-6:4).

The Lord is calling His people to walk in the fear of the Lord and in a biblical standard of holiness and purity. Marriage covenants are ordained by God and need to be honored and kept (see Prov. 16:6; Mark 10:9; 1 Thess. 4:3-8; 1 Cor. 6:18-20).

5. We are committed to spiritual families, spiritual parenting, and intergenerational connections.

Believing that our God is turning the hearts of the fathers and mothers to the sons and daughters in our day, we are committed to spiritual parenting on every level of church and ministry life (see Mal. 4:5-6; 1 Cor. 4:15-17).

Participation in a small group is a fundamental commitment to the DCFI family. The small group is a small group of believers and/or families who are committed to one another and to reaching others for Christ. We believe the Lord desires to raise up spiritual families on many levels, including small groups, congregations, apostolic movements, and the Kingdom of God (see 1 Cor. 12:18; Eph. 4:16).

We believe each spiritual family needs to share common values, vision, goals, and a commitment to build together, with the need to receive ongoing training in these areas (see Ps. 133; 2 Pet. 1:12-13; 2 Tim. 2:2).

We are committed to reaching, training, and releasing young people as co-laborers for the harvest, as the young and the old labor together (see Acts 2:17; Jer. 31:13).

6. Spiritual multiplication and reproduction must extend to every sphere of Kingdom life and ministry.

Multiplication is expected and encouraged in every sphere of church life. Small groups should multiply into new small groups, and churches should multiply into new churches. Church planting must be a long-term goal of every congregation (see Acts 9:31; Mark 4:20).

The DCFI family of churches will be made up of many new regional families of churches as apostolic fathers and mothers are released in the nations of the world (see Acts 11:19-30; Acts 13-15).

7. Relationships are essential in building God's Kingdom.

Serving others and building trust and relationships is a desired experience in every area of church life. We believe the best place to begin to serve and experience trust and relationship is in the small group (see Acts 2:42-47; Eph. 4:16; Gal. 5:13).

We are joined together primarily by God-given family relationships, not by organization, hierarchy, or bureaucracy (see 1 Pet. 2:5).

8. *Every Christian is both a priest and a minister.*

According to the Scriptures, every Christian is a priest who needs to hear from the Lord personally (see Rev. 1:5-6).

Every believer is called of God to minister to others and needs to be equipped for this work with the home as a center for ministry. Fivefold ministers are the Lord's gifts to His Church. He uses fivefold persons to help equip each believer to become an effective minister in order to build up the Body of Christ (see 1 Pet. 4:9; Eph. 4:11-12).

We need to be constantly handing the work of ministry over to those we are serving so they can fulfill their call from the Lord (see Titus 1:5; 1 Tim. 4:12-14).

9. *A servant's heart is necessary for every leader to empower others.*

We believe every sphere of leadership needs to include a clear servant-leader called by God and a team who is called to walk with him. The leader has the anointing and responsibility to discern the mind of the Lord that is expressed through the leadership team (see 2 Cor. 10:13-16; Num. 27:16; 1 Pet. 5:1-4).

Leaders are called to listen to what the Lord is saying through those whom they serve as they model servant-leadership. They are called to walk in humility, integrity, the fruit of the Spirit, and the fear of the Lord (see Acts 6:2-6; Acts 15; Matt. 20:26; Gal. 5:22-23).

We believe God raises up both apostolic overseers and partner church elders to direct, protect, correct, and discipline the church. These leaders must model the biblical qualifications for leadership (see Acts 6:1-4; Acts 15; 1 Tim. 3; Titus 1).

Those with other spiritual gifts, including administrative gifts (ministry of helps), need to be released to fulfill the Lord's vision on each level of church life (see 1 Cor. 12).

In every area of church life we believe we need to submit to those who rule over us in the Lord and esteem them highly in love for their work's sake (see Heb. 13:17; 1 Thess. 5:12-13).

10. Biblical prosperity, generosity, and integrity are essential to Kingdom expansion.

Biblical prosperity is God's plan to help fulfill the Great Commission. The principle of the tithe is part of God's plan to honor and provide substance for those He has placed over us in spiritual authority. Those who are over us in the Lord are responsible for the proper distribution of the tithe and offerings (see 3 John 2; Matt. 23:23; Heb. 7:4-7; Mal. 3:8-11; Acts 11:29-30).

We believe in generously giving offerings to support ministries, churches, and individuals both inside and outside of the DCFI family, and emphasize giving to people as a priority. We encourage individuals, small groups, congregations, and ministries to support fivefold ministers and missionaries in both prayer and finances (see 2 Cor. 8:1-7; Gal. 6:6; Phil. 4:15-17).

We believe that every area of ministry and church life needs to be responsible financially and accountable to those giving them oversight in order to maintain a high standard of integrity. Spiritual leaders receiving a salary from the church are discouraged from setting their own salary level (see Gal. 6:5; Rom. 15:14; 1 Thess. 5:22; 2 Cor. 8:20-21).

11. The Gospel compels us to send missionaries to the unreached and help those least able to meet their own needs.

Jesus instructs us to take the Gospel to the ends of the earth to those who have never heard. Our mission is to reach the unreached areas of the world with the Gospel of Jesus Christ by sending trained missionaries and through church planting. Together we can join with the Body of Christ to reach the unreached (see Matt. 24:14; Acts 1:8; 13:1-4; 2 Cor. 10:15-16).

We are also called to help the poor and needy, those in prison, orphans, and widows. This includes our reaching out to the poor locally, nationally, and internationally. When we help the poor, both materially and spiritually, we are lending to the Lord (see Deut. 14:28-29; 26:10-12; Matt. 25:31-46; James 1:27; Prov. 19:17).

12. *We are called to build the Kingdom together with the entire Body of Christ.*

Our focus is on the Kingdom of God, recognizing our small group, our local church, and DCFI is just one small part of God's Kingdom. We are called to link together with other groups in the Body of Christ and pursue unity in His Church as we reach the world together (see Matt. 6:33; Eph. 4:1-6; John 17; Ps. 133).

We wish to see God's Kingdom come not just in and through the church, but in all areas of life. We are, therefore, called to minister in the church, the family, government, the arts, education, business, and the media, so that all such spheres come under the Lordship of Jesus Christ and reflect the values of His Kingdom (see Matt. 6:10).

We believe in utilizing and sharing the resources of people and materials the Lord has blessed us with. This includes the fivefold ministry, missions, leadership training, and other resources the Lord has entrusted to us (see 1 Cor. 12; Acts 2:44-45).

Our unifying focus is on Christ, His Word, and the Great Commission, and we believe we should not be distracted by minor differences (see Rom. 14:5).

We subscribe to the Lausanne Covenant as our basic statement of faith and Christian values. The Scriptures serve as a light to guide us, and the Lausanne Covenant along with these values and guiding principles unite us as we walk together in the grace of God (see Matt. 28:19-20; Amos 3:3; 1 Cor. 1:10; 15:10).

ENDNOTES

Introduction

1.   For more about house churches, read:

Starting a House Church by Larry Kreider & Floyd McClung (Ventura, CA: Regal Books, 2007).

House Church Networks, a New Church for a New Generation by Larry Kreider (Lititz, PA: House to House Publications, 2001).

Chapter 1

1.   Harold Eberle, *The Complete Wineskin* (Helena, MT: 1989), 144-145.

Chapter 2

1.   Jim Petersen, *Church Without Walls* (Colorado Springs, Colorado: NavPress, 1992), 148-149.

2.   For more on house churches, read:

Starting a House Church by Larry Kreider (Ventura, CA: Regal Books, 2007).

House Church Networks by Larry Kreider (Lititz, PA: House to House Publications, 2001).

Chapter 3

1.   Larry Kreider, *Building Your Personal House of Prayer* (Shippensburg, PA: Destiny Image Publishers, 2008).

2.   Larry Kreider, *The Cry for Spiritual Fathers and Mothers* (Lititz, PA: House to House Publications, 2000), 4.

Chapter 4

1.   Brian Sauder & Larry Kreider, *Helping You Build Cell Churches* (Lititz, PA: House to House Publications, 2000). Website: www.dcfi.org/house2house

2.   James H. Rutz, *The Open Church* (Auburn, ME: The SeedSowers, 1992), 47.

3.   T.L. Osborne, *Soul-winning, Out Where the Sinners Are* (Tulsa, OK: Harrison House, 1980), 35-37.

4.   Howard A. Synder, *The Radical Wesley* (Downers Grove, IL: Inter-Varsity Press, 1980), 53-54.

5.   Ibid., 55-57, 63.

6.   Terry Taylor, *Perspectives,* January 1993.

7.   First Corinthians 16:2.

8.   Ralph Neighbour, *The Seven Last Words of the Church* (Grand Rapids, MI: Zondervan Publishing House, 1973), 164.

9.   Second Corinthians 3:6.

Chapter 5

1.   For more on spiritual parenting, read the books:

The Cry for Spiritual Fathers and Mothers by Larry Kreider (Lititz, PA: House to House Publications, 2000).

Authentic Spiritual Mentoring by Larry Kreider (Ventura, CA: Regal Books, 2007).

2.   *Mother Teresa: In My Own Words,* compiled by Jose Luis Gonzalez-Balado (New York: Random House, 1996), 40.

Chapter 7

1.   Larry Kreider, *What Does It Mean to Be a Real Christian?* (Lititz, PA: House to House Publications, 2007). Website: www.dcfi.org/ house2house

2.   Some of the insights about "embracing our missionaries" are from Terry Pfautz, former mission director of DCFI.

3.   This section was written by Mel Sensenig, director of a former international student ministry of DCFI.

Chapter 9

1.   *Matthew Henry's Commentary on the Whole Bible: New Modern Edition,* Electronic Database, Comments on John 1:37-42, Copyright © 1991 by Hendrickson Publishers, Inc.

2.   For more on tithing, read *The Tithe: A Test in Trust,* by Larry Kreider (Lititz, PA: House to House Publications, 2003). Website: www .dcfi.org/house2house

Chapter 10

1.   Dr. Paul Yonggi Cho, *Successful Home Cell Groups* (Plainfield, NJ: Logos International, 1981), 90, 93-94.

2.   *Small Groups 101* and *Small Groups 201* audio and DVD is available at www.h2hp.org

3.   "Growing 21st-Century House Churches and Micro Churches Seminar," presenter Larry Kreider. Churches interested in hosting a seminar may call 1-800-848-5892.

4.   For more information on the Church Planting and Leadership School, go to www.dcfi.org

Chapter 11

1. Larry Kreider & Floyd McClung, *Starting a House Church* (Ventura, CA: Regal Books, 2007), 104.

Chapter 12

1. Resources for small groups and house churches:

   Karen Ruiz & Sarah Mohler, *Creative Ideas for Cell Groups* (Lititz, PA: House to House Publications, 1996).

   Larry Kreider & Floyd McClung, *Starting a House Church* (Ventura, CA: Regal Books, 2007).

2. We recommend this marriage workbook entitled *Called Together* by Steve & Mary Prokopchak (Shippensburg, PA: Destiny Image Publications, 2009).

3. Larry Kreider, two-book series: *Discovering the Basic Truths of Christianity* and *Building Your Life on the Basic Truths of Christianity* (Shippensburg, PA: Destiny Image Publishers, 2009).

4. Ralph W. Neighbour, Jr., *Where Do We Go From Here?* (Houston, TX: Touch Publications, Inc., 1990), 204.

5. Larry Kreider, two-book series: *Discovering the Basic Truths of Christianity* and *Building Your Life on the Basic Truths of Christianity* (Shippensburg, PA: Destiny Image Publishers, 2009).

Chapter 13

1. *Emotional Dependency* and *Codependency* sections written by Steve Prokopchak. For more on emotional dependency, read Steve's booklet *Recognizing Emotional Dependency*, as well as other helpful booklets for small group leaders, available through DOVE Christian Fellowship International, Lititz, PA: House to House Publications. Website: www.dcfi.org/house2house

2. Leanne Payne, *Restoring the Christian Soul Through Healing Prayer* (Wheaton, IL: Crossway Books, 1991).

3.   We recommend this excellent resource: *Who I Am in Christ,* a tract providing dozens of Scriptures to provoke biblical change from the inside out. Order at www.dcfi.org/house2house

4.   Dr. James Dobson, *Love Must Be Tough* (Wheaton, IL: Tyndale House Publishers, 2007).

Chapter 14

1.   "Dynamic Preaching," *Net Results Magazine* (March 1991), 30.

Chapter 15

1.   Bill Scheidler, *The New Testament Church and Its Ministries* (Portland, OR: Bible Temple Publishing), 88.

2.   Kevin J. Conner, *The Church in the New Testament* (Portland, OR: Bible Temple Publishing, 1989), 110.

3.   Larry Kreider, Ron Myer, Steve Prokopchak, & Brian Sauder, *The Biblical Role of Elders in Today's Church* (Lititz, PA: House to House Publications, 2003).

Chapter 16

1.   Ron Myer, *Fivefold Ministry Made Practical* (Lititz, PA: House to House Publications, 2006).

Chapter 17

1.   Rick Joyner, *The Harvest* (Charlotte, NC: Morning Star Publications, Inc., 1989), 46.

2.   Carl George, *Prepare Your Church for the Future* (Tarrytown, NY: Fleming H. Revell Company, 1991), 51.

3.   Kevin J. Conner, *Today's Prophets* (Portland, OR: Bible Temple Publishing), 20.

Appendix A

1. *DCFI Leadership Handbook* (Lititz, PA: DOVE Christian Fellowship International, 1995, updated 2006). Website: www.dcfi.org/house2house

RESOURCES FROM DCFI

Speak Lord! I'm Listening
by Larry Kreider

Jesus said, "My sheep hear My voice," but many Christians do not know how to hear from God. In this practical, story-rich guidebook, international teacher Larry Kreider shows believers how to develop a listening relationship with the Lord. It explores the multiple ways Christians can hear the voice of God in today's world, offering real-life examples—not theory—of how God teaches His followers to listen, with tips in each chapter for distinguishing His voice from the noise of satan's interference. Christians across the denominational spectrum will develop a closer and deeper relationship with God as they learn 50 unique ways to listen to Him. You will realize that God was speaking to you all along but, like the disciples on the road to Emmaus, you didn't know it was Him!
224 pages: $14.99
ISBN: 978-0-830746-12-5

Hearing God 30 Different Ways
by Larry Kreider

The Lord speaks to us in ways we often miss, including through the Bible, prayer, circumstances, spiritual gifts, conviction, His character, His peace, and even in times of silence. Take 30 days and discover how God's voice can become familiar to you as you develop a loving relationship with Him.
224 pages: $14.99
ISBN: 978-1-886973-76-3

The Cry for Spiritual Fathers & Mothers
by Larry Kreider

Returning to the biblical truth of spiritual parenting so believers are not

left fatherless and disconnected. How loving, seasoned spiritual fathers and mothers help spiritual children reach their potential.
186 pages: $12.99
ISBN: 978-1-886973-42-8

The Biblical Role of Elders for Today's Church
by Larry Kreider, Ron Myer, Steve Prokopchak, and Brian Sauder

New Testament principles for equipping church leadership teams: Why leadership is needed, what their qualifications and responsibilities are, how they should be chosen, how elders function as spiritual fathers and mothers, how they are to make decisions, resolve conflicts, and more.
274 pages: $12.99
ISBN: 978-1-886973-62-6

Biblical Foundations for Your Life Series: Discovering the Basic Truths of Christianity; and *Building Your Life on the Basic Truths of Christianity*
by Larry Kreider

This two-book series by Larry Kreider covers basic Christian doctrine. Practical illustrations accompany the easy-to-understand format. Use for small group teachings (48 in all), a mentoring relationship, or daily devotional.
Available in Spanish!

Authentic Spiritual Mentoring
by Larry Kreider

In this book, Larry Kreider offers proven biblical keys that will open the door to thriving mentoring relationships. You will learn the Jesus Model of mentoring—initiate, build, and release—and how to apply it to the spiritual family God is preparing for you. Whether you are looking for a spiritual mentor or desiring to become one, this book is for you!
224 pages
ISBN: 978-0-8307-4413-8

Growing the Fruit of the Spirit
by Larry Kreider and Sam Smucker

This book encourages you to take a spiritual health check of your life to see if you are producing the Bible's nine exercises for spiritual wellness as mentioned in Galatians 5:22-23 and expressed in the believer as growing the fruit of the Spirit.
ISBN: 978-1-886973-93-0

Helping You Build Cell Churches Manual
compiled by Brian Sauder and Larry Kreider

A complete biblical blueprint for small groups, this manual covers 51 topics! Includes study and discussion questions. Use for training small group leaders or personal study.
224 pages: $19.95
ISBN: 978-1-886973-38-1

Church Planting and Leadership Training
(Live, in-person training or video school with Larry Kreider and others)

Prepare now for a lifetime of ministry and service to others. The purpose of this school is to train the leaders our world is desperately looking for. We provide practical information as well as Holy Spirit–empowered impartation and activation. Be transformed and prepared for a lifetime of ministry and service to others.

If you know where you are called to serve... church, small group, business, public service, or marketplace, or you simply want to grow in your leadership ability—our goal is to help you build a biblical foundation to be led by the Holy Spirit and pursue your God-given dreams. For a complete list of classes and venues, visit www.dcfi.org

School of Global Transformation
(Seven-month, residential discipleship school)

Be equipped for a lifetime of service in the church, marketplace, and beyond! The School of Global Transformation is a seven-month, residential discipleship school that runs September through March. Take seven months to satisfy your hunger for more of God. Experience His love in a deeper way than you ever dreamed possible. He has a distinctive plan and purpose for your life. We are committed to helping students discover destiny in Him and prepare them to transform the world around them.

For details, visit www.dcfi.org

Seminars

One-Day Seminars with Larry Kreider and other DOVE Christian Fellowship International authors and leaders

- How to Build Small Groups—Basics
- How to Grow Small Groups—Advanced
- Starting House Churches
- How to Fulfill Your Calling as a Spiritual Father/Mother
- Planting Churches Made Practical
- Counseling Basics
- Effective Fivefold Ministry Made Practical
- Building Your Personal House of Prayer
- How to Build Healthy Leadership Teams
- How to Hear God—30 Different Ways
- Called Together Couple Mentoring
- Starting House Churches
- How to Live in Kingdom Prosperity
- How to Equip and Release Prophetic Ministry

For more information about DCFI seminars,
Call: 800-848-5892
E-mail: seminars@dcfi.org

AUTHOR CONTACT INFORMATION

LARRY KREIDER, INTERNATIONAL DIRECTOR

DOVE Christian Fellowship International

11 Toll Gate Road

Lititz, PA 17543

Telephone: 717-627-1996

Fax: 717-627-4004

Website: www.dcfi.org

E-mail: LarryK@dcfi.org

Additional copies of this book and other
book titles from DESTINY IMAGE are
available at your local bookstore.

Call toll-free: 1-800-722-6774.

Send a request for a catalog to:

Destiny Image® Publishers, Inc.
P.O. Box 310
Shippensburg, PA 17257-0310

*"Speaking to the Purposes of God for This
Generation and for the Generations to Come."*

**For a complete list of our titles,
visit us at www.destinyimage.com.**